# LEARNING STYLES AND INCLUSION

**Dr Gavin Reid** is a senior lecturer in Educational studies at the Moray House School of Education, University of Edinburgh in Scotland, UK. He is an experienced author, teacher, educational psychologist, university lecturer and researcher. He has made over 500 conference, seminar and workshop presentations throughout the world. He has also written and edited fourteen books on areas of dyslexia and learning for teachers and parents. He is a director and consultant to the Red Rose School for children with specific learning difficulties in St Annes on Sea, Lancashire, England. He is also a consultant to a number of national and international projects in areas of special needs and learning styles and has appeared on television and radio programmes on educational matters in the UK, Europe, Asia and New Zealand. His web site is www.gavinreid.co.uk.

# *L*EARNING STYLES AND INCLUSION

Gavin Reid

Los Angeles | London | New Delhi
Singapore | Washington DC

© Gavin Reid 2005

First published 2005

Reprinted 2009

Apart from any fair dealing for the purposes of research or private study, or criticism or review, as
permitted under the Copyright, Designs and Patents Act, 1988, this publication may be reproduced, stored
or transmitted in any form, or by any means, only with the prior permission in writing of the publishers,
or in the case of reprographic reproduction, in accordance with the terms of licences issued by the
Copyright Licensing Agency. Enquiries concerning reproduction outside those terms should be sent to the publishers.

SAGE Publications Ltd
1 Oliver's Yard
55 City Road
London EC1Y 1SP

SAGE Publications Inc.
2455 Teller Road
Thousand Oaks, California 91320

SAGE Publications India Pvt Ltd
B 1/I 1 Mohan Cooperative Industrial Area
Mathura Road
New Delhi 110 044

SAGE Publications Asia-Pacific Pte Ltd
33 Pekin Street #02-01
Far East Square
Singapore 048763

**Library of Congress Control Number: 2005928101**

A catalogue record for this book is available from the British Library

ISBN 978-1-4129-1063-7
ISBN 978-1-4129-1064-4 (pbk)

Typeset by Pantek Arts Ltd, Maidstone, Kent
Printed in Great Britain by CPI Antony Rowe, Chippenham, Wiltshire
Printed on paper from sustainable forests

FSC
**Mixed Sources**
Product group from well-managed
forests and other controlled sources
Cert no. SGS-COC-2953
www.fsc.org
© 1996 Forest Stewardship Council

# CONTENTS

# ACKNOWLEDGEMENTS

Learning styles is an 'interesting and exciting' area and I am indebted to the many 'interesting and exciting' people who have contributed to bringing learning styles alive and making it meaningful in a range of learning contexts. These friends and colleagues have been my inspiration, as well as a source of sound advice and friendship. I am grateful to the staff and students at the Red Rose School in Lancashire, England, particularly my special friends Dr. Sionah Lannen and Colin Lannen, who have shown how utilising learning styles and identifying individual needs are crucial for the learning and emotional development of vulnerable students. I also wish to acknowledge the advice which has been used in this book from Stuart Lucas at Loretto School in East Lothian, Paul Bertolotto at Edinburgh Academy, Scott Meal at Davidson's Mains Primary School in Edinburgh, Fil Came of Learning Works International in Marlborough, England, Shannon Green and the REACH Learning Centre and Amanda Breslin in Vancouver, Canada, Mandy Appleyard of Fun Track Learning in Perth, Australia, Jane Healy from Vail, Colorado, Loretta Giorcelli from Sydney, whose international work is always inspiring and the long-standing advice and friendship from Dr. Barbara Given, of George Mason University in Virginia, whose inspiration initially ignited my passion for learning styles.

I also wish to acknowledge Fran Ranaldi of Kinross High School in Scotland who provided the excellent visual overviews for each chapter.

Dr. Gavin Reid

Edinburgh, Scotland, 2005

# INTRODUCTION

This book is about learning styles and inclusion. But essentially it is about learning. How to make learning more effective for all learners. To recognise the needs of learners as well as those of teachers, and at the same time appreciate that the inclusive education environment, irrespective of its merits, will present barriers for learners, and for teachers. The message in this book is that learning styles can provide teachers with an opportunity to recognise individual needs, and at the same time recognise the needs of all learners in inclusive and diverse learning environments. This book is therefore suitable for professionals and parents in every country.

It is evident that a great number of learners, for whatever reason, under perform in school. In fact there are many examples of some who have succeeded despite school and many only excel after they have left the restrictions of formal education. Surely questions need to be asked about this. As one who left school at fifteen, with no formal qualifications I am too aware of the life-long effects this can have on an individual. I am also aware, as one who developed his own learning strategies, that gaining independence and control over the learning situation is crucial for lifelong learning.

For governments and those with responsibility for education the answer lies in closer monitoring of standards, tighter control over the curriculum and more accountability all round. Yet in all this, in the midst of the debate, we have the learner. The learner is an individual, a recipient of an educational system that values standards and results. Yet many aspects of learning cannot be measured in a formal manner and those learners who do not match up to the benchmarks set by those in power are seen to be 'below standard'. Strangely, not too many studies actually ask learners why they perform 'below standard'. Why they are failing and how they would like to learn. This is what learning styles is about. It is about recognising the preferences individuals have for learning and in collaboration with learners developing appropriate learning tools, strategies, methods and materials to help them succeed.

The first chapter of this book focuses on learning and differentiates between learning and performing. It is important that young people are able to utilise the skills they acquire in learning and that they are equipped to use these skills when they leave formal education. One of the benefits of learning styles is that it can reverse the cycle of 'perceived' failure experienced by students with special educational needs. Often through the use of learning styles such students can become more effective learners and come to a realisation that their 'difficulties' are in fact 'differences'. These points are developed in Chapter 2 of this book which centres around conditions such as Attention Difficulties, Dyslexia, Developmental Co-ordination Disorders, number difficulties and children within the autistic spectrum.

In Chapter 3 the important aspect of the environment is the focus. The learning environment can facilitate learning to a great extent and it is important that more attention is paid to environmental factors in learning. Chapter 4 provides a background to the often complex picture of the different learning styles and models currently in existence. This is important because teachers can easily become confused with the range of models of learning styles and need to be clear about which approach they wish to embark on. There are many different methods of identifying learning styles and Chapter 5 contains details of some of these methods. There are also examples of observation assessment as well as student and teacher instruments co-developed by myself and colleagues. The following chapter, Chapter 6, provides examples of approaches that can be used in the classroom and reference is made to the curriculum as it is important that learning styles are set in context. The important aspect of matching teaching with learning styles is also discussed in this chapter. The book is set against the need to help students perform and fulfil their potential in an inclusive education setting. Chapter 7 provides some commentary on inclusion and identifies the key features of inclusion and its relevance to learning styles. This is developed further in Chapter 8 where some of the key issues in developing and implementing approaches to learning styles in the classrooms are considered. Examples are provided of learning frameworks, and suggestions for implementing learning styles in an inclusive classroom are provided. This chapter also considers differentiation in combination with learning styles. One of the key points here is that learning styles is more effective when implemented on a whole school basis. This point is reinforced in Chapter 9 which is on promoting effective learning. This chapter highlights how learning styles can be considered in the planning and learning process and examples are given of a range of motivating strategies for students and teachers.

Chapter 10 continues with the theme of learning strategies and also provides some personal insights from learners on how they have utilised their own learning style and strategies. This chapter also identifies the barriers that have to be overcome in order to implement learning styles in schools. The final chapter reports on the extensive range of resources, books, materials and web sites that can be accessed to help support learning in school.

I started by suggesting this book is about learning and it is important to separate learning from performance. Too often these become intermingled and the result is that learners can perform and achieve, but have little idea how they did it. Yet an awareness of learning is so important for developing lifelong learning skills when individuals are faced with new learning situations, and often without the support of teachers, or school. That is why this book is so important. Learning styles can enable students to become effective and efficient learners. This book will provide teachers with the knowledge and understanding of the importance of learning and learning styles. In the climate of inclusion an understanding of how children learn, and of learning styles, is not only desirable, but essential.

# PART 1

# HOW CHILDREN LEARN

# Learning Models and the Learning Cycle

**Outline of chapter and key points**

This chapter

- provides an overview of the different stages in the learning cycle – input, cognition and output;
- examines the learning needs of students;
- discusses factors relating to learning models;
- discusses the rationale for learning styles and inclusion.

Key points

- Distinction between learning and performance – they are not the same.
- The process of learning is important.
- It is important to identify the student's learning needs.
- One of the goals of learning is to help the student achieve autonomy in learning.
- It is crucial to ensure that the learner is presented with tasks within their Zone of Proximal Development.
- This can be achieved through the process called scaffolding.
- Awareness of learning theories such as behaviourism, cognitive theories and metacognitive theories can enhance understanding of the learning process.
- A positive self-esteem is crucial for successful learning.
- Inclusion is a process that needs to begin as early as possible and must embrace the whole community.

Education is about learning; qualifications are by-products of that learning. Yet often the reverse is the case. A school may pride itself on the number of students obtaining high grades in national examinations, but that in itself is not evidence that these students have become effective and autonomous learners. Learning is a science (and an art), and yet aspects relating to how children learn, and how learning can be used in school, beyond school and in adulthood are often relegated to a less important role in education today. MacGilchrist et al. (2004)

distinguish between learning and performance. In this context learning relates to thinking and resolving problems, while performance relates to achievement. But the skills needed for flexibility in learning and in resolving new problems may not always be evident, even among learners who have performed well. It might be suggested that performance is about the 'here and now' while learning is about the past, present and the future. In other words, effective learning will provide the learner with skills to resolve problems in new and future learning based on their previous learning experiences.

Effective learning has much to do with risk-taking. Developing new skills and new learning involves some risk on the part of the learner. Many learners are unwilling or unable to take these risks and this can result in a negative and static pattern in their learning behaviours. Watkins et al. (2002) suggest that this can form part of the learner's 'self-beliefs' about their learning abilities. They distinguish between a 'learning orientation' and a 'performance orientation' and suggest that students with a 'learning orientation' have a belief in their ability to improve and learn, have a preference for challenging tasks and develop problem-solving skills and skills in self-instruction when engaged in a task. On the other hand, a 'performance orientation' involves a need to be judged by performances, a satisfaction from doing better than others, and when the task is difficult there may be a tendency to self-evaluate negatively. Watkins et al. suggest that a 'learning orientation' is represented by a positive pattern while a 'performance orientation' can be represented by a negative pattern. The problem for schools and for learners in relation to a 'performance orientation' is that it will only be successful if the learner can actually succeed with the task. It may not be successful in dealing with new and challenging learning, unless the learner has acquired the learning skills to utilise previous learning (metacognitive skills) and to resolve the challenges inherent in new learning. This has considerable implications for learners with any form of special educational need. Often children with such needs may not have the same degree of versatility and flexibility in learning as some other children. For them it is crucial to consider the learning process and to ensure that they gain maximum benefit from this process. This theme will be developed in Chapter 2.

The performance orientation discussed by Watkins et al. underpins many aspects of the school curriculum and the examination system. The main objective within a 'content-driven curriculum' appears to be the need to obtain paper qualifications. This can relegate the learning orientation to a lesser role. In this case learning becomes a product and not a process. It is crucial, however, to consider the process of learning as well as the product, and to give serious consideration to how children learn and, specifically, how they can learn more effectively.

This chapter will therefore provide some insights into how children learn from both theoretical and practical perspectives and provide an overview of the different stages in the learning cycle – input, cognition and output. These factors will be set against the background literature on the science of learning and this will be related to classroom practice.

## Learning theory – some issues

There are many theoretical perspectives on how children learn and there are many complementary and sometimes conflicting views on learning strategies. There are however some points of general importance and consensus. These include the following:

- learning is a process;

- learning requires a period of consolidation;

- learning is more effective when the content is familiar;

- using the material to be learnt in different contexts and over time enhances the chances of retention and understanding;

- intrinsic (within child) factors as well as extrinsic (environmental) factors can influence learning;

- learning is lifelong.

Yet despite these general points there are many areas of uncertainty and controversy about learning. These include for example the view that:

- specific styles are more effective for certain types of learning;

- each person has their own style – their own 'learning fingerprint';

- learning occurs in age-related stages;

- the role of environment is less important than the individual's cognitive ability to learn;

- learning should be differentiated for children of differing abilities;

- intelligence is closely related to ability to learn.

The points above are controversial and each has been the subject of various comment and investigation by researchers and by practitioners. This chapter, in providing an overview of the learning process, will comment on these points.

## Learning needs

Before effective learning can take place it is necessary for the learner to:

- **read** the requirements of the task;

- **understand** the task/information being presented;

- **recognise** what the task, or the information is suggesting;

- **identify** the key points in the task/information;

- **implement** the task/use the information;

- **become 'efficient'** in accessing the information and carrying out the task;

- **be able to transfer** the new learning to other learning tasks.

In the identification and assessment process that takes place in classrooms it is important to focus not necessarily on the learning difficulties, but the learning needs. Often the assessment of learning difficulties takes place outside of the context of the curriculum and sometimes the classroom. It is crucial that the purpose of any assessment is seen in terms of identifying learners' needs and these should be seen in conjunction with the task that is to be undertaken. The learner therefore may have difficulty in one or all of the key points indicated above. An assessment therefore can focus on the key issues of **reading, understanding, recognising, identifying, implementing, skill development and independence in learning and transferring learning**. The situation can arise where the learner may be able to understand the task, but not be able to identify the key points, or transfer the learning that has been acquired to new learning. The learning needs that stem from this would mean that the focus of teaching would need to be on the identification of key points, summarising information and how this can be used in other contexts and subjects. The key issue is that the identification of learning needs must always be undertaken within the context of the task, focusing on the student's learning experiences with that task.

# Efficient and autonomous learning

The autonomous stage of learning is extremely important and can be seen as a measure of how successfully the individual has understood the information that has been learnt. Fitts and Posner (1967) suggest that the autonomous stage of learning occurs only after extensive practice. This practice involves the learner using the information and through this, he/she develops 'automaticity' in undertaking the task. At this autonomous stage the learner often loses conscious awareness of how the task is done and it is carried out without too much conscious thought. An example would be unlocking one's house door with a key. This task can be carried out many thousands of times, and will be done autonomously without giving too much thought to it. If a person was given the key to a friend's house with a different type of lock, however, then he/she would need to give at least some thought on how to insert and use the key. That person would still have the 'learnt skill' of using a key, but because of the differences in locks he/she may have to consciously focus more when unlocking the door. The important point is that because the individual has automaticity in using a key, he/she is able to transfer these skills to a less familiar situation. Competent learners therefore have the ability to transfer skills to new learning situations. A crucial index of learning achievement is the extent of the individual's ability to transfer learnt skills.

Nicolson and Fawcett (2004) suggest that this highlights the difference between 'controlled processing', which requires attentional control and uses up working memory capacity, and 'automatic processing', which, once learned in long-term memory, operates independently of the individual's control and uses no working memory resources. Because the learner has control over the process, he/she can be coached and trained to use this process more effectively. Almost everyone has the potential to be trained to become an efficient learner. This is one of the principal messages of this book and suggests that focusing on the learning process can help the individual gain more control over the learning experience and adopt and adapt the strategies, styles and techniques with which he/she feels most comfortable.

# Conditions for learning

It is important to give some thought to the actual conditions that can enhance learning. Environmental factors are important and these will be discussed later in this and in subsequent chapters. Other conditions can include the learner's mood, self-esteem, motivation, teaching style, materials and supports available and whether the task, or the information, is within the grasp of the learner, given his/her current level of knowledge in the area. A number of theorists have put forward ideas on the conditions for enhancing learning. Among the most well known of these ideas in terms of education is Vygotsky's 'Zone of Proximal Development'. The factors that can have an effect on learning are shown below.

## Factors that condition learning

- environment

- mood

- self-esteem

- motivation

- teaching style

- learning style

- task/task expectations

- materials

- supports

## Zone of Proximal Development

Vygotsky (1962, 1978) suggested that there can be a significant difference, at any stage in learning, between what a learner can achieve unaided, compared to the situation where there is an instructor/teacher present and interacting with the learner. Vygotsky suggested that at any moment there are some skills/knowledge that are attainable, given the learner's current knowledge at that time. At the same time some skills/knowledge cannot be accessed by the learner because he/she is not at a stage of preparedness to understand/absorb/implement these new skills or knowledge. The set of skills that are currently attainable according to Vygotsky can be described as the 'Zone of Proximal Development' (ZPD). This means that one of the key aspects of effective teaching is to ensure that the learner is presented with tasks within his/her ZPD.

## Developing ZPD

For teachers the crucial question is how a child's ZPD can be developed and extended so that new information can be absorbed and then located within the ZPD. One of the starting points is to ensure that learners are introduced to the task so that they have a clear understanding of what the task is about. Importantly the teacher needs to be aware of the learner's previous knowledge within the area to be tackled. One way to obtain this is through the procedure called scaffolding. The process of scaffolding is like a series of steps that help the learner reach the ZPD needed in order to tackle the task effectively. An example of how a learner can access ZPD through scaffolding is shown below:

---

*Accessing ZPD through scaffolding*

- Learning aim – understanding the implications of global warming.

- ZPD – Need to know the learner's previous knowledge and current skills such as:

  - reading level;

  - ability to locate informational text;

  - knowledge of

    - the location of countries with hot and cold climates;

    - factors that influence the weather;

    - industrial pollutants;

    - factors relating to structure of the universe.

*Scaffolds*

- Materials that focus on the above – maps, group work, teacher questioning, fieldwork and discussion to ensure that learning has taken place so the learner can use this for new learning. The use of reciprocal question-and-answer technique with the student. Ensure that the student has the same understanding of the task and the concepts involved as the teacher.

---

The important point in relation to scaffolding is the language of the shared communication. Essentially scaffolding involves a more skilled individual trying to impart knowledge to a less skilled person through the use of language exchange. The idea is to arrive at a shared understanding through the use of language. This is why Vygotsky suggested that the role of language is crucial to learning and to cognitive development.

## Learning theories

There are quite a number of theories of learning and these usually focus on different elements of the learning, retention and recall process. Although there can be some disagreement on theoretical perspectives on learning, there is a general agreement that children are capable of learning to a greater degree than perhaps they are credited with. Much learning is unseen and untested. The skill in learning, however, is being able to utilise learning to resolve and to illuminate current and future problems. It might be argued that the examination system can actually inhibit and restrict learning. It is important therefore to use the knowledge obtained from learning theories to assist in the planning and developing of learning plans for the classroom.

## Behaviourism

Behaviourism in relation to learning implies that learning is a behaviour that can be influenced and enhanced by other behaviours. This can be achieved through utilising 'behavioural' principles of reward and re-enforcement. Learning programmes based on behavioural principles are characterised by goals, rewards and targets. Precision learning is an example of a learning programme based on behavioural principles. This type of programme can be very useful for learners who need tasks broken down into small steps and require continual re-enforcement. The theory is that successfully completing small tasks will maintain the motivation of the learner and make the overall task more manageable. Similarly, analysing disruptive behaviour in class can be carried out using behavioural principles. This can be done in terms of antecedents, behaviour and consequences and it is hoped this type of behavioural analysis will explain the reasons for the behaviour and the possible solution.

However, there are two factors that are overlooked using these principles. These are the 'deep understanding' of the task and the individual 'learning style' of the learner.

### Deep understanding

In order for learning to be effective it is crucial that the learner obtains a deep understanding of the material to be learnt. A deep understanding will ensure that the concepts relating to the material to be learnt are fully understood and this will help comprehension and the transfer of learning to other areas and to future learning problems. Behaviourist learning models may not be able to capitalise on the deep aspects of learning and rather may provide the learner with a superficial learning experience. At the same time behaviourist principles can be used to ensure that the learner is experiencing some retention of the information and once this has been achieved further interaction can take place to ensure that deeper learning occurs.

It is worth noting that precision learning techniques and behaviourist approaches will not be suitable for all learning styles. This will be developed in more detail in further chapters but those learners who require explanations, or perhaps those who prefer to pace their own learning, may not respond well to a behaviourist model of learning.

## Cognitive theories

Cognitive theories place heavy emphasis on the processes involved in learning specific tasks. This implies that different types of tasks will incur different cognitive processes. For example, learning to read will require different processes from learning to spell, and cognitive psychologists would suggest that an understanding of these processes is crucial to understanding how the learner engages in the learning process and, more importantly, how the learning process can be made more effective for learners. This aspect within the field of psychology has had important influences over the years. This includes the stage theorist approaches of those such as

Piaget (1954, 1970), who advocated that children's cognitive development occurs in stages and that learning of new skills and concepts should match these stages. This approach is known as the constructivist approach and relates to the cognitive development of the learner. This approach was, in a sense, developed by Vygotsky (1978), who suggested that the role of the mediator (this could be the teacher) has an important influence on the learner, and this model came to be known as social constructivism. Again learning styles can play an important role in how effective these cognitive approaches will be in helping the learner fulfil their potential.

Cognitive theory usually relates to the role of information processing, and the aspects involved in processing, such as memory, organisation and neurological connections, are seen as central to this theoretical position. Burden (2002) discusses alternative cognitive models that have had an influence in education. The most well known is Feuerstein's theory of 'structural cognitive modifiability' (Feuerstein 1979). This is based upon a model of learning which incorporates the input, elaboration and output of information and the model recognises that 'deficient cognitive functions' (DCF) can occur at each phase of the learning process. Feuerstein's theory incorporates the notion of cognitive modifiability within the model to deal with these deficiencies. Burden (2002) suggests that according to Feuerstein's theory difficulties may occur at the input phase of information processing, perhaps because the learner has an impulsive learning style or may suffer from blurred or sweeping perception of incoming stimuli. At the elaboration phase the learner may be unable to discriminate between relevant and irrelevant cues in defining a problem and at the output phase the learner may not have an awareness of the needs of the recipient audience. The notion of cognitive modifiability is an important element in this theory but again the learner's learning style will be an important element in the success or otherwise of this type of intervention.

One of the key aspects of Feuerstein's theory is the Learning Potential Assessment Device. This draws on the distinction between 'dynamic' assessment as opposed to 'static' assessment. Dynamic assessment is an interactive and fluid form of assessment as opposed to traditional assessment, which is static, testing the here and now. This theory has led to a rethinking of the way in which assessment is carried out (Burden, 2002). The dynamic assessment process helps the teacher and the learner to work out an appropriate set of strategies to apply to future learning tasks and mediate how and when these might be used. This has implications for developing strategies for future learning tasks.

## Metacognitive approaches

The above model of assessment can also be described as metacognitive. This term refers to the abilities of the learner to maximise his/her learning potential. Metacognition means 'thinking about thinking' and the extent to which learners are aware of the thinking and learning processes that they are using. Three important aspects of this relate to:

- how learners can direct their learning;

- how they can monitor their learning experience;

- how they can assess the results of their learning and evaluate the learning experience.

This latter point, the learning experience, is often overlooked yet it is fundamentally important to learning. The learning experience refers to how learners feel about the learning situation and how they can use the resources and their previous knowledge to understand and access the material/skills that are being learnt.

Learners who have a high degree of metacognitive awareness

- are usually efficient and successful learners;

- have some appreciation of their own learning style since this knowledge can help to make learning more efficient;

- would ask themselves how they arrived at a particular response;

- are able to understand the information they needed to obtain that response;

- are aware of which strategies were successful and which were not;

- know how they could use specific strategies to tackle future problems.

Metacognitive approaches imply that the learner is aware of the processes that are being used and would be able to think aloud to inform the observer how the problem is being tackled. Some children, even those who obtain a correct response, are often unsure how they obtained the actual response. It is important therefore to ask learners these questions as they are tackling problems. This would help to ensure that learners are aware of the processes they are using and importantly why they elected to use a particular approach.

## Learning and self-esteem

A positive self-esteem is crucial for learning as this can provide the learner with confidence and motivation, enabling the learner with the confidence to utilise metacognitive approaches such as those mentioned above. A learner with a low self-concept will very likely have a cautious approach to learning and will have an over-reliance on the structure provided by the teacher. It is unlikely that such learners will develop a high metacognitive awareness as they will not have the confidence to become responsible for their own learning. It is important that students assume responsibility for their own learning and in time develop their own structures and eventually have the skills to assess their own competencies in tasks.

It is important that tasks, indeed all learning and learning experiences, are directed to developing the student's self-esteem. In order to develop self-esteem the learner must have some perception of success. It is obvious that if a learner is continually in a failure situation this will in turn have a negative influence on the learner's self-esteem. It is crucial that tasks are developed to ensure that the learner will succeed. This may require tasks to be broken down into manageable units. This would ensure that the learner can achieve some early success when undertaking a task and this will provide motivation for subsequent learning.

Burden (2002) refers to Kelly's Personal Construct theory (Denicolo and Pope, 2001) as a means of helping students develop an awareness of their own perception of themselves as learners. This relates to how the individual sees him/herself as a learner and, importantly, the attributions that they make for their successes and failures in learning. If learners constantly fail at learning they will attribute this failure to themselves and their lack of ability. In fact they may be failing because the task or the learning environment is not conducive to their current level of knowledge or their learning style. The attributions, that is the reasons children give for failure, are important and can provide useful information on the learner's self-perception and self-esteem. If the learner has a negative perception of their learning abilities this can give rise to feelings of low self-worth (Covington, 1992) and repeated failure can result in a situation that can be referred to as 'learned helplessness' (Smiley and Dweck, 1994). This means that the student loses motivation to learn as a result of an accumulation of failures.

It may be important to distinguish between a student's general self-esteem and their self-concept in learning. There are a number of instruments that can measure and identify this distinction, such as the Piers–Harris Self Esteem Scale, which has an academic self-concept dimension (Piers and Harris, 1964), and the Myself-As-Learner Scale (MALS) (Burden, 2000), which was developed to provide a reliable measure of assessing those aspects of a person's self-concept that are related to the learning process. Burden (1998) argues that there is a closer relationship between learning self-concept and achievement in many educational areas than between IQ and achievement.

## Implications for learning styles

All the factors discussed in this chapter have implications for learning styles. It is critical that learners are able to accept responsibility for their own learning and develop the metacognitive awareness and self-knowledge that can be acquired through recognition and use of learning styles. It is also important that teachers are aware of learning theory and how theory can be of practical use in understanding how children learn and particularly how learning can be made more accessible for learners with specific difficulties and special educational needs.

In Scotland the Scottish Executive Education Department published the Standard for Chartered Teachers (SEED, 2002). The Standard contains four key components. These are professional values and personal commitments; professional knowledge and understanding; professional and personal attributes; and professional action. Under one of these components – professional action – there is a set of criteria relating to 'effectiveness in promoting learning in the classroom'. In the document this section indicates that Chartered Teachers should 'create and sustain a positive climate for learning'. This includes action that will promote the following behaviours:

- all pupils feeling valued, supported and encouraged, and their ideas and suggestions welcomed and used;

- diligence and progress explicitly rewarded and learning is a satisfying experience;

- the classroom is conducive to maintaining learning, while fairness to all, consideration for others, good behaviour and personal integrity are reinforced;

- the cognitive and affective development and cultures of young people
  are understood.

The document also provides an explanation of what is meant by the above in the classroom situation. The document explains that teachers need to use strategies that increase pupils' learning. These include:

- having high expectations of pupils and empowering and supporting them in setting challenging, but achievable targets for themselves;

- being able to relate to and motivate learners;

- providing high-quality formative feedback, tailored to individual pupils;

- inspiring pupils and celebrating their achievements;

- relating tasks to pupils' prior learning and existing ways of understanding;

- being able to select, modify and generate curriculum materials;

- helping pupils to identify their most effective learning styles in class and out of school;

- managing effectively class, group and individual activities, and the transitions between them, where appropriate in co-operation with others.

All of these strategies are crucial for effective learning in classrooms in every country and therefore they will be commented on in some way throughout this book. It is interesting that identifying 'their most effective learning style' is explicitly mentioned and moreover it is recognised that learning style is not something that is confined to learning in the classroom, but also needs to be recognised by the student, and by others, out of school.

While it is difficult and certainly challenging for teachers to acknowledge individual children's styles in a classroom situation where a wide range of learning needs is evident, it is nevertheless crucial that some attention is paid to this. By addressing the need to acknowledge learning style, teachers are assisting students to become more aware of themselves as learners. This makes the learner more aware of how they can learn efficiently and paves the way for independent learning. This latter point is one of the key messages in this book.

## Implications for inclusion

This book has 'inclusion' in the title because effective inclusion needs to take account of the needs and differences of all children. This is the challenge of inclusion – a challenge that many teachers believe is at odds with the practical reality of meeting the needs of all learners within an inclusive setting. Yet some of the key elements of inclusion are in fact good practice in teaching and in education.

An appropriate example of this can be seen in Lousiana in the West Feliciana Parish Schools (Lindsey et al., 2004). They reported on a multidimensional model of inclusion that incorporates child health, wellbeing, school readiness, student readiness and parent training. The key elements of this model are community collaboration, student health and ensuring the student is prepared cognitively, emotionally, developmentally and socially to enter school. The authors clearly see inclusion as a developing process with the use of 'at-risk criteria for early services' as a crucial part of that process. Lindsey et al. called their approach 'right from birth', which highlights the view that inclusion needs to begin as early as possible. It also highlights the view that inclusion is a process. This point was reinforced by the Director of Children's Services and Group Director Learning and Children – a department that incorporates responsibility for education – in Gateshead in the north of England (Atkinson, 2005). She strongly indicated during a talk on inclusion that 'inclusion is a process'. It does not happen, it develops, and the younger the child is when this process develops the more likelihood there is of a successful outcome.

Inclusion also needs to incorporate the community. It is by embracing community involvement and participation that every individual can appreciate the diversity and individual qualities of others. In many respects learning styles can be equated with diversity. An example of this is the Milwaukee Partnership Academy in the United States which was created in 1999 to engage a range of significant community partners in improving the education of children by providing quality teaching and learning in the K-12 environment. The subsequent initiative, 'Sharing in Student Success', emphasised the collaborative community and required the whole community, from schools to libraries, churches and clubs, to collaborate and to provide support structures and education opportunities, including literacy programmes, to the youth of the community. This community-wide involvement can be characterised by its potential proactive solution to the challenges that can be experienced in an urban community school system.

It is within this situation that learning styles need to be considered. Learning styles are about individuality and diversity in much the same way as inclusion. The challenge of inclusion, however, often means that individual needs are not as fully considered as they should be. Learning styles can therefore be a vehicle for ensuring that the individuality of all learners is paramount, particularly within an inclusive educational environment.

The following chapter discusses some of the individual differences children can show in their cognitive abilities in learning. There are a number of ways of meeting these needs. Sufficient staffing in the classroom is certainly one way, but the practical reality firmly suggests that most teachers will have to cater for the range of learners within the classroom by accessing the available supports. The supports available to teachers will vary from classroom to classroom, but the responsibilities of individual teachers will be the same.

There has been criticism in the research literature on learning styles (Coffield et al., 2004). Nevertheless, conventional wisdom suggests that if one can identify a child's learning preferences and ensure that there is scope for meeting these preferences within the classroom, the potential learning experience and outcome should be enhanced. This could have implications for resources, the nature of the tasks that are set, supports and the environment of the classroom. Noting the learning preferences of individual children and ensuring that the classroom environment caters for a wide range of learning preferences can greatly assist the teacher to ensure that an inclusive educational experience can be a reality for all learners.

## Chapter 1 Overview
# Learning Models and the Learning Cycle

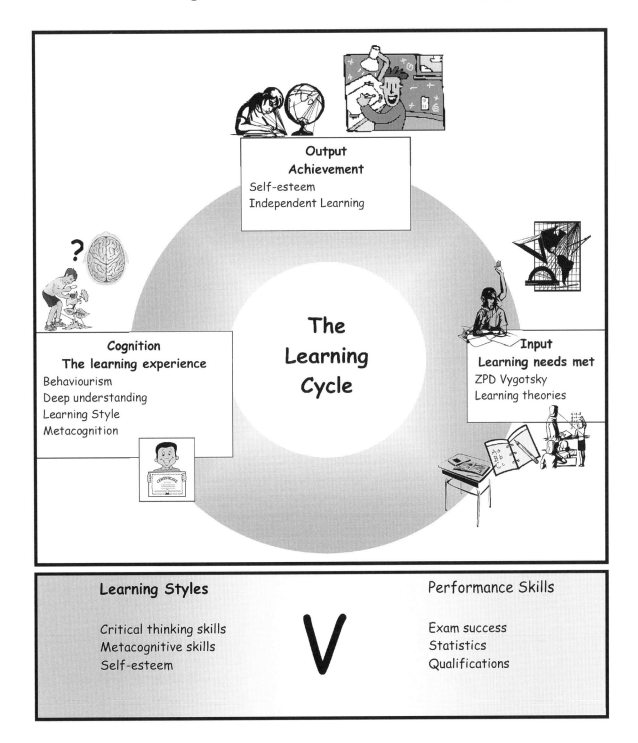

**Output**
**Achievement**
Self-esteem
Independent Learning

**Cognition**
**The learning experience**
Behaviourism
Deep understanding
Learning Style
Metacognition

**The Learning Cycle**

**Input**
**Learning needs met**
ZPD Vygotsky
Learning theories

**Learning Styles**

Critical thinking skills
Metacognitive skills
Self-esteem

**Performance Skills**

Exam success
Statistics
Qualifications

HAPTER 2

# Learning Differences and Learning Styles

> **Outline of chapter and key points**
>
> This chapter
>
> - discusses the learning differences experienced by learners with special educational needs;
> - examines some strategies using learning styles for learners with special educational needs and provides an overview of different conditions such as ADHD, dyslexia, developmental co-ordination disorders, number difficulties, children within the autistic spectrum;
> - examines these factors against the context of inclusion.
>
> **Key points**
>
> - Do we have the right type of expectations for students with special needs?
> - Organising the classroom environment and understanding cognitive and learning styles can help children with special needs learn more effectively.

This chapter describes and discusses the differences between learners, particularly those who may be considered as having special educational needs. Students who do have special needs are usually quite vulnerable in some learning situations and can have difficulty in adapting to different teaching styles and teaching environments. Learning styles therefore can have a key role to play in helping to consider the most effective learning environment for students with such needs. The role of learning and learning styles as influential factors on educational outcomes for students with special educational needs will be discussed in this chapter.

## Why learning differences?

This chapter is called 'learning differences' for a reason. It could just as easily have been called learning difficulties, or disabilities, but these terms presuppose that the challenges and the difficulties are due to the student. Yet this need not be the case: the difficulty experienced by the student could just as easily be due to the expectations of the exam system, or the approaches to teaching as well as the learning environment. Changes to any of these may bring about different results and minimise or ameliorate the 'special needs'. It is appropriate therefore to perceive students with special needs not in terms of deficits, disabilities or even difficulties, but in terms of differences.

It is the role and the responsibility of the education system, the school and the individual teacher to ensure that these differences are catered for within the system. This is a tall order and perhaps an idealistic desire, but the key point is that it represents an attitude shift and such a shift is necessary if teachers are to be able to accommodate to the range of differences within most classrooms today. I was particularly touched when, at the feedback session after a talk I gave to all the staff of a school in Perth, Western Australia, almost all subject heads indicated how they could make their classroom more learning-friendly to meet the diverse needs of children. This included accommodating to those students who were seen as having 'special educational needs'. Within twenty-four hours the physics department had rearranged the physics classrooms to take account of the different learning styles in the classes. This highlights the fact that changes can be made easily and quickly. It is possible for an attitude shift to be made and a realisation on the part of the teacher that it is possible to meet diverse needs in a class by accommodating to and recognising different learning styles. This further emphasises the need to explain and perceive learning difficulties in terms of differences rather than disabilities.

## The spectrum of differences

The following section of this chapter will discuss a range of syndromes that are usually seen within the context of 'special educational needs' and highlight how learning styles can help students and teachers in the classroom context. Many of these have been developed and extended by Weedon and Reid (2003) in the development of the instrument known as the Special Needs Assessment Profile (SNAP; www.SNAPassessment.com).

## Attention disorders

### Characteristics

It is important to recognise that syndromes such as attention disorders are usually seen within a continuum from mild to severe. Nevertheless, there are some key characteristics that are usually noted in students experiencing difficulties associated with these syndromes. Some of these associated with attention disorders are:

- difficulty in attending and maintaining attention in most areas and in most tasks;

- easily distracted;

- may process information superficially, rather than in depth;

- students showing ADHD can be impulsive and often have a lack of impulse control;

- they can show a degree of hyperactivity, but the extent of this may vary – the hyperactivity should be recognised within the learning context; it can also be displayed as 'multi-tasking', where the student has a need to focus on several different stimuli at the same time, which can be the student's own way of dealing with the attention difficulties.

# Strategies using learning styles

## Classroom environment

- Organising the classroom environment is important and it may be preferable if the student is seated near the front of the class, and certainly close to the teacher's desk.

- Specially designed desks that can minimise distractions – for example, desks with sides.

- Variety of working areas – it is important that the student has a variety of work areas and it may be necessary to change the work environment to suit the task.

- Group work is important but it should be carefully managed to ensure that the student with attention difficulties is grouped with others who are understanding of this and can help to bring out the strengths in the student.

## Cognitive style

- Students with attention difficulties will have difficulty in sustaining attention and therefore may have short-term memory difficulties. It is important that only one piece of information is presented at any one time. Providing too much information at once will confuse and frustrate the student.

- It is preferable to provide a series of short tasks with frequent breaks.

- Students may respond to a behavioural approach that involves goal-setting, as long as the goals are realistic and attainable.

Students with ADHD may process information at a shallow as opposed to a deep level. This is because they do not spend sufficient time on one topic or task to facilitate deep processing. It is useful to develop strategies that can help with depth of processing. Setting the student specific types of question relating to the item that is being learnt can do this. 'Why' and 'comparison' questions can be useful as they will persuade the student to think about the topic more deeply. The writing frames and the metacognitive approaches developed by Wray (2002) can be useful for this. Wray shows how the following can be used in writing frames:

- argument;

- contrast;

- comparison;

- discussion;

- persuasion;

- sequence.

**Example of writing frames to help with depth of processing**

## Argument

I think that _____ because _____ .

The reasons for my thinking this are, firstly _____

_____ .

Another reason is _____ .

Moreover _____ because _____ .

These (facts/arguments/ideas) show that _____ .

Some people think that _____ because

they argue that _____ .

## Discussion

Another group who agree with this point of view are _____ .

They say that _____

_____ .

On the other hand _____ .

disagree with the idea that _____ .

They claim that _____ .

They also say _____

_____ .

My opinion is _____

_____ .

Because _____ .

(Adapted from David Wray's website (2004); www.warwick.ac.uk/staff/D.J.Wray/Ideas/frames.html)

## Other suggestions

- All students need positive feedback, but students who have attention difficulties may need more reinforcement through positive feedback than others. It is important for that reason to set realistic and achievable goals so that positive feedback and success are a likely outcome.

- It will also be useful to provide an indication of the positive aspects to parents as this will be a further source of reinforcement. Some types of learners obtain motivation from extrinsic sources such as parents and teachers.

- Many students with ADHD are global, right-brained learners. It is likely they will respond well to the use of colour, and colour can be used to help develop strategies for organisation and to help with short- and long-term memory.

## Metacognitive style

As discussed in the previous chapter, metacognition is an important element for successful and effective learning. It can be particularly useful for helping in the transfer of learning. Students with ADHD may have the potential to use effective metacognitive strategies but be unable to access these strategies because of interference from other factors, distractions and difficulty in sustaining attention. It is important to bear this in mind and if the student does have a metacognitive style he/she will want to discuss facts and prefer to investigate the reasons for an event. Enquiry-based learning will be the most effective and this can also be suitable for many students with attention difficulties in general. It is important, however, to impose some form of framework to ensure that the area the student is investigating is structured and they have some form of plan. An example of this is shown opposite. A framework such as this will help with the metacognitive aspects of planning, predicting and organising.

## Framework for an investigation

### TASK–Building a bridge

- What type of bridge is to be built?
- What is it made of?

**Planning**
(underline: relating to task)

- What kind of materials will I need?
- Who is it for?
- How can it serve the purpose?
- What will be the best materials for the purpose?

**Predicting**
(underline: relating to plan)

- Length of time task will take.
- How will I know I have completed task successfully?
- What are the expectations?
- How many in the group?

**Organising**
(underline: relating to process)

- What are the roles of each person?
- Where will we get the materials from?
- Will there be any cost involved?
- How will we record what we are doing?

The framework relates to the task, the plan and the process. All these factors are part of the metacognitive planning that needs to take place before students commence a task such as the one in the example. The student with ADHD may have difficulty in undertaking this process and will need to work with others. This highlights the benefit of group work but it must be ensured that the composition of the group is positive and constructive to ensure that the student with ADHD will be able to use his/her skills effectively.

*Emotional style*

There are many different factors that can relate to emotions, emotional needs and emotional style. Students with ADHD may have an emotional need to be part of a group but as indicated above, the construction of the group is important. It is also worth remembering that because students with ADHD often do not process information deeply they may not obtain much emotional satisfaction from the learning experience. Follow-up discussion therefore can help to develop interest and also provide the student with some emotional satisfaction and success. Success, above all, is the important factor in relation to the student's emotional development.

Similarly, encouraging hobbies and outside interests will also generate emotional wellbeing in the student. Such interests may also help with friendships and the importance of this for students with ADHD should not be minimised.

# Dyslexia

## Characteristics

Dyslexia is a difficulty in processing information that mainly affects the development of literacy. Other characteristics of dyslexia include:

- difficulties in effectively utilising short- and long-term memory;

- difficulty in processing information at speed;

- organisational difficulties;

- phonological difficulties;

- visual difficulties in relation to visual acuity and visual scanning;

- co-ordination difficulties;

- difficulties in utilising metacognitive strategies;

- difficulty in the development of automaticity.

It should be noted that dyslexia can occur within a continuum from mild to severe and that not every individual will display the same characteristics to the same degree. For that reason it is important to consider the individual learning style when developing a programme and in organising the learning environment. This is clear from the following definition of dyslexia, particularly the reference to the individual learning and work context.

*Dyslexia is a processing difference experienced by people of all ages, often characterised by difficulties in literacy, it can affect other cognitive areas such as memory, speed of processing, time management, co-ordination and directional aspects. There may be visual and phonological difficulties and there is usually some discrepancy in performances in different areas of learning. It is important that the individual differences and learning styles are acknowledged since these will affect outcomes of learning and assessment. It is also important to consider the learning and work context as the nature of the difficulties associated with dyslexia may well be more pronounced in some learning situations. (Reid, 2003)*

## Strategies using learning styles

### Classroom environment

Many of the adaptations suggested for ADHD may be suitable for students with dyslexia. This can include particularly the following:

■ Utilising a range of classroom environment layouts – a quiet corner is necessary for some tasks and a work table for group tasks. It is important that the student with dyslexia feels included within the environment.

■ The environment should be stimulating and provide the students with a sense of ownership. One way of achieving this is to ensure that the children have some control over the wall display and that the children's work features to a great extent in the wall display.

### Cognitive style

In the main students with dyslexia usually have a right-hemisphere processing style. This means that they will prefer to process information visually and holistically. In relation to teaching this would mean that they will prefer an overview of the information, or the task to be tackled first, before setting about tackling the individual components of the task. In terms of teaching reading this would mean that first they would need an overview of the story line, the main characters and the general context before embarking on reading the book. Other suggestions from a cognitive perspective include:

■ providing one task at a time to ensure that it has been understood and consolidated before embarking on the next task;

■ allowing additional time to complete tasks;

■ helping the student develop effective long-term memory strategies for retaining and recalling information; this may be through using a visual approach.

### Metacognitive skills

It is important to ensure that the student is able to access metacognitive skills. This is important for reinforcing learning and for ensuring that appropriate concepts and schema have been developed by the student. This will develop comprehension and help with the transfer of learning. It will also assist the student to use previous learning experiences to understand new learning. This can also be achieved in the following ways:

- through interaction and question/answer techniques with the student;

- by encouraging the student to monitor and assess his/her own work;

- by providing the student with opportunities to develop his/her own plan for the task that is to be tackled;

- through guiding the student to self-question when tackling new learning in order to ascertain what exactly the task is asking, if this type of task has been tackled previously and, if so, what strategies were used then and how successful these strategies were.

Developing metacognitive skills with students with dyslexia is essential. It can provide them with responsibility for their own learning and help to make learning more effective. As with ADHD, many students with dyslexia will have a weakness in metacognitive awareness and need to be provided with a structure and a clear picture of the task that is to be carried out (this aspect is discussed in later chapters in Part 4 of this book). The problem-solving skills of students with dyslexia can very often be excellent. Often, however, they need to be shown how to access these skills; in other words, how to tackle questions and topics, and in order for that to be achieved they may need some form of structure or question/answer interaction with the teacher.

West (1997) has championed the cause of the giftedness of dyslexia. He discusses evidence that the same brain differences that are associated with dyslexia can be positively linked to some of the giftedness and special talents seen in many dyslexics. He suggests that the 'general observation has been that individuals who are especially talented in visual/spatial modes (sculptors, painters, architects, engineers, designers and film-makers should not be surprised when they (and their close family members) have difficulties with some aspect of a mostly word-dominated educational system – especially in the early years' (West, 1997, p271). There are clear implications here for the recognition and the use of learning styles. In relation to the above there is little point in teaching a young dyslexic child in an auditory and linguistic manner. It is important that children who are dyslexic and who show strong visual/spatial abilities are taught to these strengths. Healy (1994) illustrates that difficulties in one area of learning should not prevent success in another. This is extremely relevant in the case of children with dyslexia. Visual processing skills and problem-solving skills that can be evident in students with dyslexia can help to overcome the obvious language and sequential processing difficulties dyslexic children often experience. Reid (1996) describes this as accessing the 'other side of dyslexia' and shows how West highlights the alternative means of processing and accessing information by people with dyslexia. West explains how the explosion of learning materials in the visual/spatial area has benefited dyslexic people, but also helped to change attitudes to learning from a rigid, narrow traditional focus to an inventive, flexible and imaginative one. The implication is that children with dyslexia may perform less well in tasks that require sequence and logic than in those tasks that require innovation and creativity. West summed this up extremely well when he said:

*We ought to pay less attention to getting everyone over the same hill using the same path. We may wish to encourage some to take different routes to the same end. Then we might see good reasons for paying careful attention to their descriptions of what they have found. We may wish to follow them some day.* (West, 1991, from Reid, 1996, p491)

This not only emphasises the need to encourage children with dyslexia to utilise their learning style but also recognises that we as teachers and adults may learn something from listening to what they have to say about learning.

### Emotional style

Many children with specific learning difficulties can be sensitive, particularly in relation to learning. This needs to be acknowledged and these students will greatly benefit from positive feedback and praise. Useful activities include the following:

- Circle time, which encourages everyone to be accepted and held in positive regard by peers through games and activities that encourage empathy and mutual understanding.

- Recognising the need to boost self-esteem. This can be achieved by ensuring the student with dyslexia achieves some form of success and that he/she is aware of the fact that they have been successful. In order for self-esteem to be enhanced the student will need to experience some success or receive some form of positive feedback. Positive feedback can relate to virtually anything and need not only be related to the student's area of difficulty. For example, students with dyslexia can have good social skills and this can be used to highlight their strengths. If this is the case, this should be related back to students so that they recognise and appreciate their strengths. This will be useful for future learning and can help to develop a positive self-concept.

# Developmental co-ordination difficulties

## Characteristics

Developmental co-ordination disorders (DCD) are characterised by poor motor co-ordination. This could be fine motor processing such as the skills needed for writing and drawing and/or gross motor difficulties that can affect balance and general body movement. Developmental co-ordination disorders are usually associated with the condition called dyspraxia and although dyspraxia can be noted within a continuum, other factors such as organisation, language development, literacy and processing speed can also be affected. Reid (2005a) suggests that DCD, like so many of the other specific learning difficulties, are not a homogeneous group.

Portwood (2004) reports on the study by Gueze et al. (2001), who reviewed 164 publications on the study of DCD and found that only 60 per cent were based on objective criteria. Jones (2005) reports on individuals with DCD and shows how their difficulties can affect not only learning but their self-image and social skills. One person she reports on was only diagnosed at university, but once he realised his difficulties and was empowered to take responsibility for his own learning he became an effective and successful learner. Jones suggests that the problem is not only related to the child area of difficulties, but can be seen within much broader issues concerning the emphasis on the academic disciplines that currently dominate the curriculum, despite other developments in learning. She suggests that initiatives such as Gardner's Multiple Intelligence theory (1999), which considers logical, musical, spatial and interpersonal dimensions equally within the learning environment, should be utilised for children with developmental co-ordination disorders.

## Strategies using learning styles

### Classroom environment

For students with DCD it is important to make some effort to ensure the classroom environment is organised in a manner that will be conducive to effective learning. It is worthwhile considering the following:

- Background noise may be distracting; therefore the student with DCD may focus more effectively if he/she is seated near the front of class.

- Open-plan classrooms may be beneficial as they will provide students with DCD the space that they probably need for moving around, but at the same time classrooms organised in this way can be distracting. If the classroom is open plan then every effort should be made to ensure there are some quiet and enclosed areas that can help individual students to work with minimal distraction.

- The gym can be a good environment for students with DCD because there is usually a lot of space for movement and physical education, as a subject, can be useful and perhaps therapeutic. It is important to note, however, that students with DCD may be lacking in skills in sports and other games. Yet it is important to make effective use of the physical education time. The PE class should be designed in a user-friendly manner with some smaller areas for individual or small-group activities that the student with DCD can experiment in without experiencing undue embarrassment.

It is interesting to reflect on some of the comments made by children with DCD (Stephenson, 2000): 'It doesn't matter how hard I try I never win'. 'It's no use – I just can't do it'. 'It's always too difficult.' 'My hands forgot what to do.' 'Everything in the world is boring – the playground is the most boring of all.' This last comment sums up much of the frustration that can occur for children with DCD and particularly the resulting de-motivation.

### Cognitive style

In a similar way to the dyslexic processing style, the student with DCD will have difficulty carrying out several tasks at the same time. The cognitive style needs to be appreciated when teaching and planning class work. For example, students with DCD may have difficulty in:

- listening and writing at the same time;

- understanding and following a sequence of instructions;

- retaining information in short-term memory.

Students with DCD/dyspraxia will therefore benefit from short tasks and frequent breaks.

### Metacognitive style

Although DCD principally relates to co-ordination factors, other aspects such as those involving metacognitive skills can also be affected. Planning ahead and self-organisation therefore can be challenging. The student would therefore require a structure. At the same time, however, over-structuring should be avoided as this may have an adverse affect on self-confidence. This can also be counter-productive in terms of developing the independence and confidence necessary to acquire metacognitive skills.

### Emotional style

Sport and team games are held in high regard with students generally and those who excel in these are usually very popular with peers. The nature of the difficulties associated with DCD means that team games and sports can be a potential disaster area. Yet they are very much part of youth culture and it is important that students with DCD are accepted by peers. Every effort needs to be made to help such students find at least one sport they can participate in without their co-ordination difficulties becoming too obvious. There is now a much wider variety of sports and games played in school so it should be possible to do this. This is important because students can derive considerable benefit from sport and activities involving games of any sort.

Although students with DCD will differ in their learning style, most will very likely be quite sensitive in relation to their difficulties. This means they will need positive feedback and the type of praise that can make them feel worthy and more secure emotionally. Participation in sports for pleasure rather than for competition will be preferable and at the very least they can be praised for their participatory role.

## Number difficulties

### Characteristics

Many students have difficulties with numbers. This can be called dyscalculia. It involves a weakness with calculation and number bonds. These are usually arithmetical and the student may also have difficulty with the sequential processes involved in maths. There may also be difficulty coping with the memory demands which can accompany mathematical problems and additionally with the literacy demands involved in some areas of maths.

## Strategies using learning styles

*Classroom environment*

Maths is a subject that often requires the student to concentrate for fairly lengthy periods. This can be threatening and frightening for the student with dyscalculia and it is important that the classroom environment is organised in such a manner that such students are within sight of the teacher. This would mean that the teacher would be able to notice if the student was experiencing stress or facial tension and could therefore intervene.

The student with dyscalculia will also need classroom space for experiments and perhaps need to use 'concrete' objects to assist in the working out of calculations.

*Cognitive style*

One of the principal areas of difficulty can be working memory. This means that rote memory of times tables and learning formulae will be challenging. Strategies to deal with this should be discussed with the student. If the student has a right-hemisphere thinking style then he/she may have difficulty with some of the mathematical operations that require precision. The student will also need the teacher to break problems down into several steps.

*Metacognitive style*

It will be necessary to allow additional time for the student to check, and monitoring the progress through the various steps. The teacher can of course do this but it is important that the student takes some responsibility for this aspect of learning as it will help in the development of metacognitive skills.

It is also important that students with dyscalculia understand the question and the task. If they have low metacognitive awareness they may easily misunderstand the question, particularly if they have already a fear of mathematical problems. It is crucial therefore that the technical language of maths is minimised and certainly at least explained. Even commonly used words such as 'evaluate' and 'product' can cause difficulty because they have other general meanings outside of the mathematical context.

*Emotional style*

Students with mathematical difficulties may very likely have strengths in other areas. It will be useful if these areas can be identified so that the student can obtain positive feedback and reinforcement from these areas. Nevertheless, maths is important and every effort should be made to provide the student with dyscalculia opportunities for success within maths. This can be done through group work as the different tasks can be divided within the group and the student with dyscalculia can take responsibility for a task that he/she can do without too much difficulty. This sharing of the task can be useful for students with maths difficulties and can result in them feeling more emotionally secure in the area of maths.

Although it is important to ensure that there are minimal distractions for students with dyscalculia, Henderson et al. (2003) suggest that background music can be beneficial as it can stop the mind from wandering, block out other noises and prevent boredom. They suggest that familiar music is better as it means that students do not have to stop and listen.

Some specific maths activities and particularly maths games can be very useful, such as those from Crossbow Education (www.crossboweducation.com). They specialise in games for students with such difficulties and produce activities on numeracy. These include *Oh No*, a times-table photocopiable game book, and *Tens 'n' Units*, a series of spinning board games which help children of all ages practise the basics of place value in addition and subtraction. Similarly, the book *Working with Dyscalculia* (Henderson et al., 2003) contains a rich source of pupil activities. This book also recognises the emotional side of dyscalculia and provides some pupil comments on 'how to teach'. These include 'lots of both oral and practical work', 'large desk with space to work', 'looking at board straight on and not sideways' and 'good displays on pinboard' (p120). Similarly, Butterworth and Yeo (2004) indicate that teachers need to provide positive learning experiences for dyscalculic students. They suggest the following: being positive and supportive, giving students time to think, making maths sessions varied, structuring the difficulty of work, ensuring that students have appropriate support, including clear model examples. Games and activities, it can be suggested, are a way of communicating with students with dyscalculia. This is a less threatening way to deal with the problems of maths and can have a fun element. The book *Dyscalculia Guidance* (Butterworth and Yeo, 2004), like the book by Henderson et al., contains a wealth of games activities for students with dyscalculia.

# The autistic spectrum

## Characteristics

There are a number of characteristics that can be seen within the autistic spectrum. These include social awareness and language communication as well as difficulties in social, interpersonal and emotional awareness. There may also be evidence of obsessive and inappropriate behaviours. Some students within this spectrum may also have limited imaginative thought. The condition known as Asperger's syndrome can also be noted within this spectrum.

## Strategies using learning styles

### Classroom environment

It is important to create a calm, predictable and consistent working environment. Students within the autistic spectrum will find change difficult, and will not be able to deal with unexpected change in the classroom. It may also be useful to keep arousal level low and minimise sensory distractions. Such students can be particularly sensitive to noise and some types of flashing visual stimuli. A subdued sensory environment can therefore have the most calming effect on students within the autistic spectrum.

It is also important to allow for opportunities that will enable the student some time on his/her own. Although socialisation is important, a balance will need to be provided within the environment that will enable the student to have time to reflect and relax, but still have opportunities to be part of a group and to work with at least one other in some tasks.

## Cognitive style

Structure is important: activities need to be highly structured and in some cases closely supervised. It will be necessary to interact with the student and this should be done calmly and sensitively. The student will obtain security from structure and predictability and this should be built on and extended into a wider variety of activities.

The language that is used in the teaching and learning situation should be kept simple and effort should be made to ensure that the student has understood exactly what has been meant. One of the difficulties experienced by students within the autistic spectrum is the difficulty in recognising and understanding inferences, that is information that is implied rather than explicitly detailed. It is necessary to detail information precisely so that there is no doubt at all what is meant and that there is no room for ambiguity and misunderstanding.

Students with autism and Asperger's syndrome usually have limited ability to interpret social cues so this should not be relied on too much as a means of communication. It is important, however, that these cues are practised and that gestures and other body language communication are practised as these form an important area of the total communication. It may therefore be useful to use pictorial and visual cues to supplement oral communication.

## Metacognitive style

One of the essential aspects of metacognitive awareness is that the student can make inferences and judgements about what is being asked for in the task and how the task should be carried out. Clearly this will present a significant difficulty for students within the autistic spectrum. This is in fact one of their principal weaknesses. It is important nevertheless to try to establish this and aspects such as independence, decision-making and change should be encouraged, but sensitively and slowly. Much of this depends on the actual difficulties and how disabling these are for the student. It is particularly important to consider the student's emotional security and this should be paramount.

## Emotional style

As indicated above, the emotional security of the student is important and effective learning is more likely to take place if the student feels secure about the learning environment. It is also important that the expectations placed on the student are realistic but at the same time some students have considerable ability and potential and this should be maximised whenever possible.

In addition to language and communication difficulties, students within the autistic spectrum will try to avoid uncomfortable social situations. Although some effort should be made to introduce gradual acceptance of social situations, any avoidance needs to be understood and accepted. It is important therefore that no unnecessary pressure is placed on the student to participate in social situations.

# Implications for learning style

This chapter has discussed a number of well-known syndromes and indicated that it is important to recognise the need to understand the students' learning styles within the background of the particular pattern of difficulties (and strengths) associated with each of the syndromes discussed.

It is also important to recognise that students with the same label will be different, and firstly they should be viewed as individuals. This means that as well as considering the most appropriate types of learning environments and styles that will be beneficial for them it is also necessary to understand their individual personality and learning preferences.

## Learning differences and inclusion

There is now a great thrust towards inclusion in virtually every country. This can present real challenges to teachers and others involved in the education process, including parents. One of the ways of dealing with this has been the increase in professional development and providing teachers with information on these syndromes, which previously were exclusively within the domain of specialists. This is beginning to change and some countries are much further along that road than others. But it is crucial that in the desire to obtain information and details about the characteristics and the nature of these syndromes the use of labels to describe these syndromes does not dominate the intervention that is to be used. Macintyre and Deponio (2003) discuss the advantages and disadvantages of using labels. They recognise that although a label can help to access resources, provide a description of the difficulty, bring relief to both children and parents and identify the most appropriate strategies, it can also be limiting and misleading for some children. To ensure this does not happen it is important that learning styles – one of the most fundamental aspects to consider in planning the learning and teaching context – are given a high priority.

It can be argued that inclusion can become a reality if learning styles of all students are placed higher on the agenda. It is important that a teacher does not describe his/her class as consisting of two dyslexics, three students with ADHD, one dyspraxic, two students with dyscalculia and one student within the autistic spectrum. Rather the teacher should describe the class as individuals who can be best catered for, not in relation to the syndrome, or the label they carry, but in terms of their individual learning preferences. The knowledge teachers gain about the syndrome will help in the planning and teaching as well as in the organisation of the classroom. This needs to be set against the information obtained on the student's individual learning style. This can make the whole concept and the challenges inherent in achieving inclusion less daunting and indeed more realistic for the teacher.

# Chapter 2 Overview
# Learning Differences and Learning Styles

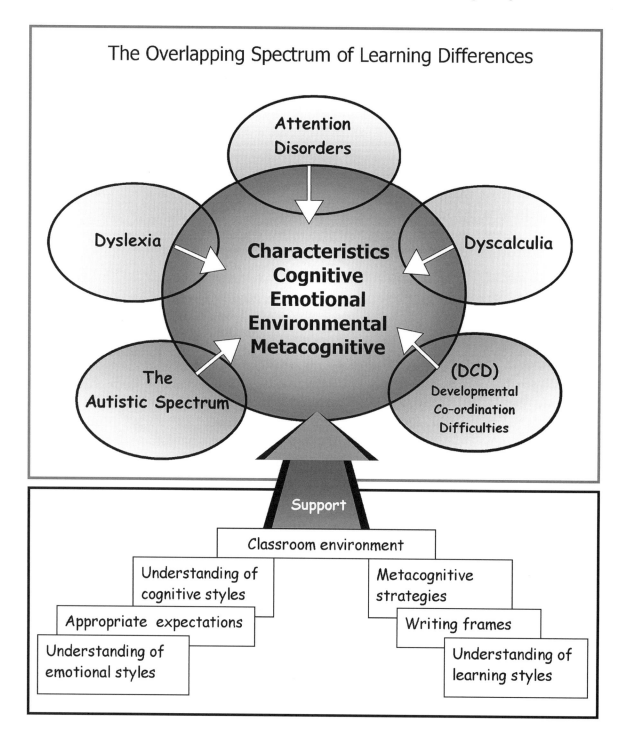

The Overlapping Spectrum of Learning Differences

Attention Disorders

Dyslexia

Dyscalculia

Characteristics
Cognitive
Emotional
Environmental
Metacognitive

The Autistic Spectrum

(DCD)
Developmental
Co-ordination
Difficulties

Support

Classroom environment

Understanding of cognitive styles

Metacognitive strategies

Appropriate expectations

Writing frames

Understanding of emotional styles

Understanding of learning styles

# The Role of the Learning Environment

**Outline of chapter and key points**

This chapter

- highlights the importance of the environment for learning;
- suggests that the role of the learning environment is underrated; and
- shows how the learning environment can influence performance and emotional wellbeing.

Key points

- The classroom design and layout should try to accommodate to features associated with learning styles – such as colour, sound and music and general design.
- Some learning environments may be more suited to left-hemisphere learners and others to right-hemisphere learners. Some examples are provided in the chapter.
- Environmental preferences can be considered following discussion with the learner or through observation of the learner in different settings.

The learning environment is perhaps one of the most underrated features in the learning process. Environmental factors contribute to the learning experience a great deal and can significantly increase or decrease the effectiveness of learning. Many learners are not aware of this and often just accept the environment as it is, without making any attempt to manipulate it in any way. In some instances it can be difficult to make a choice, or to change the environment at all. But this is not always the case and if learners are aware of their environmental preferences then they are in a position to make informed choices when they do have some flexibility over learning. In most cases, certainly for younger learners, the learning environment refers to the classroom, but it can in fact refer to the other areas that are used for learning, such as the library and home study. The environment is very influential and should be seen as an important resource that can help access effective learning for all students.

The key aspects in the learning environment will be discussed in this chapter and how different environments can be more suited to certain types of learning styles. This will highlight the view that the learning environment can to a great extent influence learning.

# Key environmental considerations in the classroom

There are a number of factors that need to be considered in relation to the learning environment. These include:

- design;
- colour;
- wall displays;
- light;
- sound;
- visual and auditory distractions;
- space;
- the presence of other learners in the same environment.

# Design

The design of the classroom, or learning environment, cannot be taken lightly. In most cases the key factor is cost, but this should not take precedence over the need to meet the individual requirements of users. In most classrooms there will be a range of needs to be met and it is likely that there will be students with some of the recognised disabilities such as those outlined in Chapter 2 – dyslexia, developmental co-ordination disorder, attention difficulties and the autistic spectrum as well as those learners with sensory deficits such as hearing and visual impairment. The classroom design therefore should take account of these factors and ensure that the layout and design of the classroom are not only teacher-friendly, but also learner-friendly.

Some of the factors that can be considered are:

- layout – the organisation of classroom furniture;
- the design of chairs and desks;
- the position of the teacher's desk in relation to the students;
- the arrangement of the students' desks;
- the flexibility in being able to move and adjust the layout of the classroom;
- location of the classroom in relation to other classrooms in the school;
- colour and shape of the room;
- amount of light;
- amount of available space.

Although they will not be discussed here, health and safety requirements also need to be considered.

## Design – Implications for learning styles

As indicated above, the design of a classroom is very important and can do much to make the learning experience more effective for many learners. Auditory learners may prefer a classroom design with space and only a few items organised in an orderly fashion. Some types of learners gain security from order and predictability. A room design that is constantly changing might cause disruption for some learners.

Some types of learners, again particularly auditory learners, will prefer desks to be in a conventional layout and will prefer sitting in an upright chair when learning. Others, particularly global, right-brained learners, will prefer an informal classroom design and may even prefer to sit on a cushion on the floor rather than an upright chair. It is therefore important to be flexible in the arrangement and the design of a classroom. This would mean that a number of different preferences can be accommodated. Ideally the design should not be fixed and there should be scope for adaptations depending on the preferences of the current students in the class.

Some learners prefer to know exactly where the teacher will be located – some like to be seated near the teacher, others prefer to be more distant. It is important to acknowledge these preferences as there are usually reasons why some learners have these particular preferences.

Classrooms can be 'closed' or 'open'. The teacher's preferences can come into this and some teachers prefer to have an open door when teaching. This can also be beneficial for some children who do not like experiencing feelings of being enclosed. Others of course prefer to work in a quiet and closed-door environment.

While it is difficult to cater for all the preferences of all the learners in the class, it is possible at least to be aware of these preferences and to attempt to introduce some flexibility so that it will be possible to accommodate to most learners some of the time. Nevertheless, Figures 3.1 and 3.2 show the differences in classroom layout over the years and indicate that there has been progress! The progress, however, is more related to the choice and the opportunities teachers and school managers have for redesigning classrooms. The picture of the traditional style desks (Figure 3.2) is from an era when it was not expected that there would be any choice, and furthermore the classrooms were designed to be teacher-centred. The modern picture (Figure 3.1) is from a new school where the school managers decided and planned how the classrooms should be designed. They did this bearing in mind the needs of the learners. The school is for children with specific learning difficulties and it is designed so that there are opportunities for private space as well as group work. The teacher's space and desk are virtually nonexistent.

**Figure 3.1  A modern classroom (courtesy of Red Rose School, Lancashire)**

**Figure 3.2 A mid twentieth century classroom**

# Colour

Colour is an important factor in learning. There has been some recent emphasis on colour therapy, and the effect of colours on the health, mood, attention and general alertness of people has been well documented in the popular press and magazines. Colour therapy is one example – this is a professional procedure that aims to balance and enhance the body's energy centres by using the seven colours of the light spectrum, which can help to stimulate the body's processes (www.colour-therapy.co.nz, www.colourtherapyhealing.com).

As far back as 1932, Gerrard and Hessay, two Californian psychologists, scientifically established that:

- blue light has a calming effect;

- red light has a stimulating power on human beings.

Blue and red colours are considered at the two extremes, with yellow representing the midpoint. These are also the three principal colours in a rainbow (www.peacefulmind.com/color_therapy.htm).

It is therefore claimed that colours and colour combinations have a profound effect on one's well-being and so it is not surprising that people can be affected by colour in a learning environment.

The Irlen syndrome, also known as scotopic sensitivity, is an example of how people can be perturbed by glare, sunlight, headlights or streetlights. Some can experience discomfort or difficulty concentrating and working under bright lights or fluorescent lights. Some individuals become tired, others experience headaches, mood change, become fidgety or have an inability to stay focused with bright or fluorescent lights (Irlen, 1991; www.irlen.com). This, it is claimed, can affect school work and particularly reading and concentration.

It is important therefore to consider the following in the classroom:

- colour of classroom furniture;

- colour of classroom walls;

- range of colours in wall displays;

- views from window;

- colour of paper, books and others materials and the containers for these materials.

## Colour – Implications for learning styles

Colour has an influential effect on most people. Colours can stimulate, subdue, elate or depress individuals. Pastel colours are usually a safe bet and these colours can be conducive to learning. It may not be possible to give individual students complete choice over colour schemes, although if this is possible it should be done, but students can have some choice over the colour of their own learning resources and should be allowed to use their preferred colour whenever possible.

# Displays

Wall displays are very significant in the learning environment. They can tell much about the nature of the learning that is occurring and visual displays can have an emotional impact as well as an informative one. Some of the factors that need to be considered include:

- content of wall displays;

- visual appearance of displays;

- organisation of wall displays and other types of displays;

- quality of displays;

- ownership of wall displays.

The example of a wall display in Figure 3.3 highlights many of these factors and indicates also that the children have focused on their own learning preferences.

**Figure 3.3 A wall display on learning (picture courtesy Paul Bertolotto, Edinburgh Academy)**

## Displays – Implications for learning styles

This is particularly important as wall displays can reflect the nature of the work and the results of the students' work. The content of wall and other displays is important. Most learners like to see their work displayed and this can generate both pride and confidence. Some of course may not want to see this and if this is the case it can provide a valuable opportunity to investigate why this should be so. It may be due to the learner having a low self-concept, or perhaps the learner's self-perception is not a realistic one and he/she is unduly and unrealistically critical of the work that has been completed.

How wall displays are organised is also quite important – the choice between placing almost all noteworthy work on the wall or just a selection needs to be considered carefully. Competitive learners may feel under some pressure if there is an element of selection when deciding on exhibits for the wall – this can be overcome by introducing a rotation system.

Wall displays can be informative and can be seen as an extension to the lesson. This can be useful for independent learners who want to develop the topic on their own after the lesson.

# Light

Light and in particular natural light can have a significant effect on people. The condition known as Seasonal Affective Disorder (SAD) can cause depression in some people during the winter months. It is postulated that melatonin, a sleep-related hormone secreted by the pineal gland in the brain, has been linked to SAD. This hormone, which may cause symptoms of depression, is produced at increased levels in the dark. When the days are shorter and darker the production of this hormone increases (see www.nmha.org/infoctr/factsheets/27.cfm).

It can be suggested therefore that the amount of both natural and artificial light can have an impact on learning. When planning and reorganising the learning environment the range, amount and quality of light need to be appreciated. Factors that can be considered include:

- the size and the arrangement of the windows;

- the outside view;

- the type of lighting in the classroom and the students' opportunities for changing the lighting to suit individual preferences.

## Light – Implications for learning styles

Everyone is affected by light. Some prefer, and in fact need, a considerable amount of light, while others can be quite indifferent to this. But light can stimulate and excite. It is important that there are some 'light' areas in the classroom with natural light if possible and some areas where the lighting is more subdued. This would cater for different types and allow the undertaking of different tasks.

Windows are important, and again there should be a variety of seating arrangements that can allow both visual stimulation, if the outside view is conducive to this, and areas where outside distractions are kept to a minimum.

The kind of lighting is also an important consideration. Very bright fluorescent lights may not be the best lighting for learning. Students who are sensitive to some environments and have a right-hemisphere approach to learning may prefer dim table lights rather than glaring fluorescent lights.

# Sound

Sound can be one of the most distracting elements in learning. At the same time it has the potential to stimulate, invigorate and create. People react differently to different sounds and this needs to be considered in a learning environment. There has been a great deal of interest in the role of music in learning, both in terms of listening to music and actively playing a musical instrument. For example, it has been suggested that soft music in the nursery, musical toys and dance lessons, encouraging music involvement in a fun way, strengthens children's educational, physical, and emotional development. It can be argued therefore that one of the best ways to enhance children's learning with music is to encourage listening to and learning music  throughout the child's developmental years (http://childparenting.about.com/cs/k6education/a/ mozarteffect.htm).

The term 'Mozart effect' was coined after publication of research that students who listened to the Mozart Sonata in D Major for Two Pianos had short-term subsequent enhancement of their spatial–temporal reasoning (www.mindinstitute.net/MIND3/mst/overview.php).

The research from the MIND Institute Research Division in California discovered the link between music, the brain and spatial reasoning. Additionally, researchers from the MIND Institute, Graziano et al. (1999), demonstrated that pre-school children given six months of piano keyboard lessons improved dramatically on spatial–temporal reasoning, while children in appropriate control groups did not improve. It was then predicted that the enhanced spatial–temporal reasoning from piano keyboard training could lead to enhanced learning of specific maths concepts, in particular proportional maths, which the researchers claim is notoriously difficult to teach using the usual language-analytic methods.

The Canadian Association for Music Therapy/Association de Musicothérapie du Canada in Vancouver, British Columbia, defines music therapy as the 'skilful use of music and musical elements … that can promote, maintain, and restore mental, physical, emotional, and spiritual health. Music has non-verbal, creative, structural, and emotional qualities. These are used in the therapeutic relationship to facilitate contact, interaction, self-awareness, learning, self-expression, communication, and personal development' (www.musictherapy.ca/definition.html).

This association suggests that listening to music has many therapeutic applications and can help to develop cognitive skills such as attention and memory and provide a stimulating environment for exploration and understanding.

This point is reinforced by Anderson et al. (1999), who suggest that Baroque music helps learners focus and perform better. They suggest that Baroque music uses only one melody and the brain relaxes in the assurance that it knows what is happening with the music. A key aspect of this is the relaxation element as all learners will perform better and recall information more effectively when they are in a relaxed state. Anderson et al. also suggest that the particular combinations of rhythms of Mozart can stimulate creative right-brain areas and can 'cause the brain to go into action, connecting different cells and creating connective pathways between different parts of the brain' (p68).

Factors that need to be considered in the environment in relation to sound include:

- the background sound in the classroom;

- the type of sound;

- if music is to be used, what kind of music;

- the sounds outside the classroom and the school.

## Sound – Implications for learning styles

Most sounds in a classroom can be monitored and manipulated. It may be necessary to provide headphones for some children who need musical stimulation, whereas others may need a quiet environment. It is worthwhile allowing some children to use headphones and monitor the output of their work when using background music. It is important to experiment with different kinds of music. A quiet corner can also be provided in a classroom for those children who need it. It is misguided to equate silence with productivity. Noisy classrooms can in fact be extremely productive and stimulating for the learners.

# The learning environment

Frederickson and Cline (2002) suggest that there is substantial literature which supports the importance of the learning environment. This can support the view that environmental factors can account for differences in performances in examinations, school attendance, motivation and the development of learning skills. Student attitude, as well as achievement, can be enhanced by paying careful attention to factors within the classroom environment. This indicates that the learning environment is crucial, particularly in relation to learners who may have difficulties in acclimatising to different teaching styles, and particularly for children with learning difficulties.

Some established theoretical models showing the importance of environmental factors in learning have already been influential in education. Many of those have advocated a systematic approach to the assessment and development of the learning environment (Bandura, 1977; Bronfenbrenner, 1979). Wearmouth and Reid (2002) report on the influence of Bronfenbrenner's model. They indicate how the learning environment can produce barriers to pupils' learning. The ecosystemic perspective developed by Bronfenbrenner (1979) can be a useful guide to this. It identifies four levels that influence children's learning outcomes:

- the **microsystem** – the immediate context of the child – school, classrooms, home, neighbourhood;

- the **mesosystem** – the links between two microsystems, e.g. home–school relationships;

- the **exosystem** – outside demands/influences in adults' lives that affect children;

- the **macrosystem** – cultural beliefs/patterns or institutional policies that affect individuals' behaviour.

This system indicates that the learning environment needs to be considered and the implication is that an assessment of the students' needs must be comprehensive and include all aspects of the system described above as each can influence the educational outcomes. This point cannot be over emphasised, particularly as there may be a tendency to focus on narrow environmental and cognitive factors in an assessment, particularly with children with special needs.

Dockrell and McShane (1993) suggest that the environment and the interaction of the environment with the learner are crucial as well as the task to be undertaken. An analysis of the interaction between the learner and the environment can provide a helpful guide for the teacher and this type of analysis can have particular implications for students with learning difficulties. Often for children with learning difficulties the interactive role in learning can be particularly important as many children with learning difficulties do not have self-sufficiency and flexibility in learning and rely to a great extent on the structured interaction with the teacher and the environment. Understanding the importance of the environment and of the teacher's role in helping the learner utilise the environment can minimise the effects of a learning difficulty and enhance performance and self-esteem. It is for that reason that a learning styles perspective that includes the learning environment, as well as a focus on the curriculum and teaching approaches, can hold the key to helping all children learn effectively, particularly vulnerable children who are at risk of failing.

An understanding of the importance of learning styles should be an influential feature in a school's daily practice, its policy and its philosophy. In order for learning styles to be effectively implemented they need to be incorporated into a whole-school perspective and policy. This will make it easier for individual teachers to incorporate into their daily teaching. Classrooms therefore need to be designed with learning styles in mind. For example, as indicated earlier in this chapter it may be necessary to redesign seating arrangements or to provide students with a choice of desk styles. It is also important to give careful consideration to other classroom environment factors such as furniture, design, light, sound, colour, space and the general ambience of the class or school.

Some examples of this are shown below by indicating different types of classroom environments and how these may impact on learning.

# Classroom environments

## The 'mind your table manners' classroom

This type of classroom will be very much teacher-directed and students will have little control. They will be very aware of classroom rules and may feel apprehensive and perhaps restricted in this type of environment. At the same time, for some students it can be ideal. There will be a high degree of predictability and this can be suitable for some.

*Benefits*

- predictability
- routine
- students are aware of class rules
- the structure can be good for some

*Disadvantages*

- excessively controlled by the teacher
- lack of freedom
- heavily based on routine
- can be difficult for learners who prefer an informal learning environment

## The 'set menu' classroom

This type of classroom environment can be quite predictable and the learners will know where everything can be found. Perhaps there are set corners for different items – for example, there may be a news corner, an area showing students' work, a story corner and quiet work area. This can be a secure and predictable environment and can be well suited to some learning styles.

*Benefits*

- secure and predictable environment

- easy to locate items

- all resources can be easily accounted for

- students will know where the teacher will be seated

*Disadvantages*

- can be very much teacher controlled

- may be a lack of freedom for exploratory learning

- heavily based on routine

- can be difficult for the learner who prefers an informal learning environment

*Implications for learning styles*

This type of environment can be beneficial for students who prefer the teacher to take control and prefer the teacher to structure work for them. It can also be beneficial for students with learning difficulties as there is a degree of predictability about the classroom layout. Some children, particularly those with learning difficulties, find it difficult to adapt to change. Additionally, because the teacher has considerable control in this environment, there is a greater chance that items will be easily accessible by the students and the teacher will be in a position to assist students locate information and resources more easily.

## The 'à la carte' classroom

This type of classroom is an extension of the 'set menu' one described above. The main difference is that there will be fewer items on display and there will be a degree of competitiveness. Again there will be a pattern to how items are displayed and the layout of the classroom can be visually appealing.

*Benefits*

- can be a visually appealing classroom to work in

- easy to find items

- good if student needs structure

*Disadvantages*

- can be difficult for informal learners

- can instil a degree of competitiveness and inequity

*Implications for learning styles*

As in the previous description, the à la carte classroom will have some pattern and predictability. This will be useful for some types of learners. There might, however, be a degree of competitiveness and only the best work will be displayed. This can be discouraging for some students. Additionally this can be a fairly formal type of classroom environment and some global learners who prefer an informal learning situation may find this difficult.

## The 'buffet' classroom

This type of classroom (see Figure 3.4 below) is characterised by the amount of visual stimulation. Usually when entering this type of classroom the visitor is overwhelmed by the amount of displays. The displays need not be confined to the wall but can cover ceiling, door and perhaps even the windows. Like a buffet, everything is on display and the visitor has to select the aspects that they find particularly interesting. It can be a highly stimulating environment for many students and teachers. The resources are usually on display and the students help themselves to what they need. The teacher's desk is virtually nonexistent.

**Figure 3.4 A classroom with high level stimulation**

*Benefits*

There are many advantages in this type of classroom:

- visually appealing;

- children's work usually displayed;

- students can note and more readily recall the work they have completed;

- provides students with sense of ownership and responsibility;

- stimulating environment.

*Disadvantages*

- may be over-stimulating for some students

- some children may not have as many wall displays as others

- takes up a lot of teacher time

*Implications for learning styles*

This type of classroom environment can incorporate a range of styles. It is important that the needs of those students who require quiet and prefer working on their own are considered. This type of environment may also provide additional problems for children with spatial orientation difficulties such as those sometimes evident in students with dyspraxia. There is a greater chance that all learning styles can be incorporated in this type of learning environment.

## The 'street market' classroom

This type of classroom is best described as 'very busy'. Virtually everything is in sight and it can be visually stimulating for some. For others it might resemble chaos. The students also have a great deal of responsibility in this type of classroom and may feel free to bring in their own materials and leave them for others to see. There appear to be few rules on how items, desks and other materials are organised. Nevertheless, this type of classroom can be conducive to high functioning work and the students may benefit from the informal classroom arrangements.

## Benefits

- visually stimulating

- informal design can be suited to some

- students have a sense of ownership

- work is readily and quickly displayed in some way

*Disadvantages*

- can be chaotic for some

- may also be disorganised and finding items can be difficult

- can be frustrating for students who prefer predictability

## Continuum of classroom environments

The five examples shown in this chapter have been deliberately grouped in this sequence. They range from the classroom environment that would be most suited to left-hemisphere students who prefer structure and predictable environments, to the more global right-hemisphere students who prefer an informal environment and a great deal of visual stimulation.

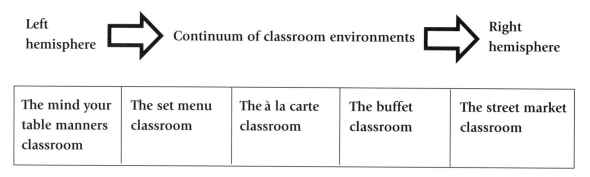

The examples in this chapter highlight that all types of classroom design can have beneficial features in relation to a learner's style. It is helpful, however, if the teacher has an indication of the type of styles shown by the students in the class. This could provide some information to help in the planning of the classroom layout and learning environment. Manipulation of the learning environment is certainly one way to incorporate the range of learning styles that can be found in today's inclusive classrooms. This can be just as important as the attention that is usually given to preparation of teaching materials and curriculum and task differentiation. All these factors are important and can all contribute to ensuring that the diverse needs of all learners are met.

## Environment and stress

There is little doubt that some environments can be stressful. For some learners noisy environments can be disturbing while for others this type of environment may actually be stimulating. It has been demonstrated that some environments can stimulate and can influence the development of learning (Diamond and Hopson, 1989). Following on from their study at the University of California at Berkeley, these researchers suggest that an enriched environment for children should include:

- a steady source of positive support;

- a nutritious diet with enough protein, vitamins, minerals and calories;

- stimulation of all the senses (not necessarily at once);

- an atmosphere free of undue pressure and stress;

- a series of novel challenges that are neither too easy nor too difficult for the child;

- social interaction for a significant percentage of activities;

- an atmosphere that promotes the development of a broad range of skills and interests: intellectual, physical, aesthetic, social and emotional;

- an opportunity for the child to choose tasks and to be able to adapt these;

- an enjoyable atmosphere that promotes exploration and the fun of learning;

- opportunities for the child to be an active participant rather than a passive observer.

Many of the above points are basic requirements for an enriched environment. In addition to this, the particular preferences of the learner need to be considered. One of the key aspects to consider is the potential to provide the learner with choice. While it is good to encourage flexibility in the application to learning tasks in different environments, it should be noted that some learners will not be able to learn effectively in certain types of classrooms and environments. It is for this reason that environmental preferences should be considered. This is best achieved following discussion with the learner or observation of the learner in different settings. This can apply to very young children as well as to adults and is one of the central considerations in applying learning styles in the classroom.

# Chapter 3 Overview
# The Role of the Learning Environment

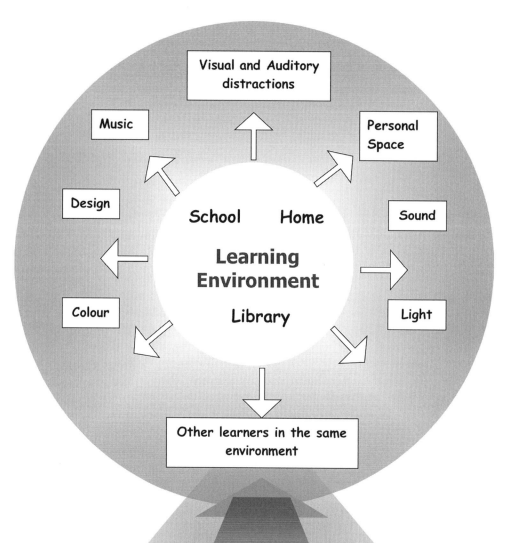

PART 2

# LEARNING STYLES

# Background to Learning Styles

**Outline of chapter and key points**

This chapter provides

- an overview of the literature on learning styles;
- a summary of a number of examples of models of learning styles such as Kolb's experiential learning model, Honey and Mumford's learning styles approach, the Dunn and Dunn model and Given's five learning systems;
- and some answers to questions on the implications for teaching and learning of using learning styles in the classroom.

Key points

- There are at least 100 instruments designed to identify individual learning styles.
- These instruments tend to focus on modality preference, social situations, cognitive processing, personality types, emotional factors and lateral preferences.
- Factors that can influence learning styles include culture, school climate, expectations, teaching style and classroom practices.
- There has been some criticism of learning styles in the scientific literature, mainly due to the lack of reliability in some instruments that claim to measure learning styles and the controversy over whether matching individual learning styles to teaching styles and teaching materials does actually produce more effective learning.
- Learning styles can overlap and complement other aspects of learning such as multiple intelligence, metacognition, thinking styles and teaching styles.
- Knowledge of learning styles can help the student become more aware of individual preferences and can lead to metacognitive awareness.
- Acknowledging learning styles can help to promote skills that can extend beyond school.

This chapter will provide a summary of the background literature on learning styles. Although there are a number of studies supporting the different theoretical and practical positions relating to learning styles, the research field is still characterised by controversy and in many instances by its criticism of the use of learning styles (Coffield et al., 2004). Some of these controversial issues will be discussed in this chapter. Nevertheless, despite these controversies, it is strongly advocated in this book that the use of learning styles in the classroom can help teachers deal with many of the challenges they face in inclusive schools.

Given and Reid (1999) suggested there are at least 100 instruments designed to identify individual learning styles. A recent study by Coffield et al. (2004) identified 70 learning styles instruments. Attempts have been made to categorise these instruments to show the background influences and the psychological and cognitive perspectives of the different styles.

Given and Reid (1999) suggested that these instruments usually focus on factors that are seen to have some influence over the learning process. These factors include:

- modality preference: the preference for visual, auditory, tactual or kinaesthetic input;

- personality types, such as intuitive, risk-taking, cautious and reflective;

- social variables, including the need to work alone or with others;

- cognitive processes, such as memory, comprehension and methods of information processing;

- movement and laterality, such as active learning and left- and right-hemispheric activities;

- emotional factors which can be incorporated in many of the above categories such as personality and social preferences.

Coffield et al. attempted to group 71 learning styles models into some form of classification in order to make sense of the range of instruments and perspectives that contribute to these models. They developed a continuum of models based on the extent to which the developers of these models believed that learning styles represented a fixed trait. At one end of the continuum, Coffield et al. placed theorists who believed that learning styles were fixed by inherited traits, and at the other end they placed those theorists who focused more on personal factors such as motivation and environmental factors as well as those theorists who acknowledged the influences of curriculum design and institutional ethos and culture.

At various points throughout the continuum Coffield et al. placed models, like Dunn and Dunn's model (see later in this chapter), that acknowledge external factors, particularly the immediate environment, and models that are based on the idea of the dynamic interplay between self and experience.

For the purposes of this book it is suggested that learning styles could be grouped in the following ways – those that focus on:

- personality styles;

- environmental influences in learning;

- cognitive styles;

- metacognitive influences.

Over and above those factors, all styles of learning are mediated by:

- the learner's culture;

- the classroom and school climate;

- teaching style;

- classroom dynamics and environment;

- the curriculum and school expectations.

These factors are highlighted in the diagram below.

**Learning Styles**

**Influences**

Personality
Environment
Thinking style
Self-awareness

**Mediating factors**

Culture
School climate
Expectations
Teaching style
Classroom practices

The implication of this diagram is that the mediating factors can influence the factors that determine learning style but at the same time those factors can also influence the mediating factors. This means, for example, that the learner's thinking style can be affected by the teaching style, while at the same time teachers can adapt their teaching style to fit in with the learner's thinking style. The key point is that learning styles and the variables that affect learning styles need not be fixed. Learning is a fluid process and learners and teachers can accommodate to one another, to a certain extent, throughout the learning process.

## Learning styles critique

There has been some criticism of the concept of learning styles. The criticism rests on a number of key issues. These include:

- the lack of reliability seen in some of the learning styles instruments;

- the competing perspectives on learning styles, even among supporters of the concept;

- the notion that it is impractical to adhere to the individual learning styles of all children in a class;

- the controversy on whether matching individual learning styles to teaching style and teaching materials does actually produce more effective learning;

- the commercial element that often accompanies a particular learning styles perspective. Sometimes to implement a specific approach teachers need to attend a training workshop and purchase expensive materials.

As a result, the learning styles approach does not always have a sound image in the educational psychology literature. However, it will be argued here that this is mainly due to a misunderstanding of the purposes and in particular the underlying conceptual understanding of learning styles, certainly as it is applied in the classroom situation. Some theorists see learning styles as a fixed, perhaps genetically determined, trait like size and hair colour. Using this type of criterion it is not surprising that instruments do not stand up to scientific scrutiny. It is well known that environmental influences are very powerful in determining a young person's characteristics, both in terms of learning and behavioural factors. Learning styles are therefore no exception to these influences. One is treading on dangerous territory therefore when attempting to ascribe a learning style to an individual as a fixed trait. Additionally it needs to be recognised that many, indeed most, of the instruments measuring learning styles are based on self-report. This method of obtaining data relies heavily on the individual's awareness and accuracy in identifying their awareness of their preferences. If the descriptions based on questionnaire responses were seen as a guide rather than an accurate and absolute picture then the questions being put forward in any scientific scrutiny would be qualitatively different. The key questions should not relate to an investigation of an instrument in isolation, but to the value of the data obtained by that instrument in guiding classroom learning, teaching and curriculum development.

One of the key questions therefore is *should learning styles be seen as a fixed set of criteria?'* Some learning styles proponents argue yes, it should, but common sense and years of classroom experience suggest that children have learning preferences, but these are only preferences and are not necessarily fixed. Certainly some children may have a more refined learning style than others, but this is perhaps because they have less of a repertoire of preferences to fall back on and have to cling narrowly to the only way they can learn. The danger is that when opportunities to use their preferred style are not available they may fail in the learning situation. Adhering to learning preferences therefore can prevent children from failing, particularly vulnerable children. This is particularly important in an inclusive educational context where it can be very challenging to cater for the needs of all.

As author of this book I recognise and accept the controversy that surrounds learning styles and appreciate the dangers of narrowly adhering to a specific approach/perspective or instrument to measure learning style. Although the title of the book includes 'learning styles', the perspective throughout the book is on learning preferences, how these preferences can be used to identify a particular learning style in children and, importantly, about acknowledging that an effective learning environment needs to incorporate a range of stimuli that can be accessed by all learners. This supports the view that children in every classroom will show a variety of styles and preferences. Using this rationale it is possible to cater for the diversity teachers have to cater for within an inclusive classroom.

Coffield et al. (2004) evaluated 13 major models of learning styles. These included:

- Allinson and Hayes' Cognitive Styles Index (CSI);

- Apter's Motivational Style Profile (MSP);

- Dunn and Dunn's model and instruments of learning styles;

- Entwistle's Approaches and Study Skills Inventory for Students (ASSIST);

- Gregorc's Styles Delineator (GSD);

- Herrmann's Brain Dominance Instrument (HBDI);

- Honey and Mumford's Learning Styles Questionnaire (LSQ);

- Jackson's Learning Styles Profiler (LSP);

- Kolb's Learning Style Inventory (LSI);

- Myers–Briggs Type Indicator (MBTI);

- Riding's Cognitive Styles Analysis (CSA);

- Sternberg's Thinking Styles Inventory (TSI);

- Vermunt's Inventory of Learning Styles (ILS).

(See the Appendix for web links to the major models.)

Coffield et al.'s evaluation commented on a previous evaluation (Curry, 1987). Curry's evaluation suggested that researchers in the field had not yet established unequivocally the reality, utility, reliability and validity of these concepts (relating to learning styles). The Coffield et al. review showed in fact that these problems are still evident.

Curry's evaluation (1987, p16) suggests that *'the poor general quality of available instruments* [makes it] *unwise to use any one instrument as a true indicator of learning styles … using only one measure assumes* [that] *that measure is more correct than the others. At this time (1987) the evidence cannot support that assumption'.*

Coffield et al. suggest that one of the important aspects to emerge from their review was the importance of context. The important role of context in learning will be discussed throughout this book as it can justify the need to perceive learning styles within a practical teacher-developed framework. It purports the need to contextualise instruments, to provide frameworks and guidance on learning styles for specific learning contexts. An instrument therefore should be used carefully and perhaps cautiously, but that does not necessarily rule out the validity of using learning styles in classroom practice. Even a brief period of observation can provide the teacher with information on the child's style that can be useful in planning, in differentiation and in the delivery of the curriculum. This will be covered in later chapters.

Some of the issues raised in the critique of learning styles by Coffield et al. can be levelled at most forms of tests or classroom measures. Even measures such as those that focus on reading can be deemed controversial because the outcome can vary depending on the nature of the reading task and the type of reading skills that are being measured (Shiel, 2002). Shiel commented on the IEA[1] Reading Literacy Study (IEA-RLS), the OECD[2] Programme for International Student Assessment (PISA), and the IEA Progress in International Reading Literacy Study (PIRLS) and noted that a number of test construction and measurement variables could affect the outcome of such assessments of reading skills.

Similar factors can influence the measurement of learning styles and this underlines the fact that instruments need to be used judiciously and the purpose of the instruments and the learning context in which they should be used made clear. The main aim of such assessments is to inform the teacher in order that he/she will be more aware of the learning preferences of the children in the class.

[1] IEA: International Association for the Evaluation of Educational Achievement, based in Hamburg, Germany.
[2] OECD: Organisation for Economic Co-operation and Development, based in Paris, France.

Stahl (1999) provides a summary of learning styles studies, most of which fail to demonstrate the value and the effectiveness of adopting a learning styles approach. For example, Snider (1992) found difficulties in reliably assessing learning styles and a lack of convincing research that such assessment leads to improvement in reading. Snider suggests that test–retest reliabilities are particularly important for a measure of learning styles and the reported reliabilities of most measures are relatively low. Snider suggests that this can mean that the learning styles assessment is not measuring what it intends to measure, or how in fact the students' learning styles may change. In either of these situations Snider claims an assessment of learning styles can be problematic. He also claims that children make progress not by adhering to their learning style but through effective teaching and curriculum development. That, he claims, has nothing to do with learning styles.

## Learning styles overlap

One important factor to consider is the overlap between learning styles and other important aspects of learning. There can be some connection between learning styles and the following areas of interest:

- learning theory;

- learning strategies;

- thinking styles;

- multiple intelligence;

- cognitive style;

- metacognition;

- teaching style.

This list will be familiar to some extent to most teachers but because each area has different meanings and interpretations, understanding what is meant by each of the above may give rise to confusion. Often the differences between them are quite subtle and this might be confusing for the teacher who essentially wants to be informed about the best way to teach to obtain maximum understanding from the learner. The list above can be collapsed to read 'learning preferences'. Using a term such as learning preferences means that the teacher is not labelling the child with a 'style' or 'type' which in itself can take the form of a label.

For clarification, however, a brief explanation of the terms that can be associated with learning styles or learning preferences is shown below.

### Learning theory

This relates to the processes of learning and how the learner interacts with the material to be learnt. Usually this relates to cognitive psychology and so is discussed using different models of learning. Such theory can sometimes help to explain learning differences and learning difficulties.

## Learning strategies

This refers to how the learner manages learning. A learner may have the skills to learn but strategies will support him/her and assist him/her to respond in a more efficient manner. Knowledge of strategies can make the difference between success and failure in a learning task. Strategies are about the ability of the learner to know how to apply his/her abilities to the task. Learning strategies are like tactics for learning. In the same way that a football coach can provide a football team with tactics to win a game, even when the opposition is seen to be vastly superior to the team, a learner can equip him/herself (or be equipped) to develop tactics or strategies for learning – even for material that is seen to be beyond their understanding.

One of the problems with the traditional examination system is that learners who have developed skills in examination tactics can do well and the examination result can in fact not represent the learners' actual abilities in that area.

## Thinking styles

Sternberg (1997) suggests that thinking styles describe the preferred way of using abilities. Sternberg suggests that the predictive power of intelligence/ability tests accounts for around 20 per cent of school performance. Sternberg puts forward the view that thinking styles may account for the 80 per cent unexplained variation in school performance. He suggests that people think in different ways and this can be described in terms of a profile of styles. It is suggested that styles of thinking can take the same form as styles of government. Sternberg and Wagner (1991), in the *Thinking Styles Inventory*, argue that thinking styles can be explained in terms of the following:

- functions – legislative, executive and judicial;

- forms – monarchic, hierarchic, oligarchic and anarchic;

- levels – global, local;

- scope – internal, external;

- leanings – liberal, conservative.

Legislative students enjoy doing things the way they decide to do them. They therefore prefer problems that are not pre-structured for them. Their style may not be totally compatible with the format and the expectations in examinations. Sternberg suggests that some entrepreneurs succeed because they are legislative and want to create their own way of doing things. Sometimes in schools legislative people can be viewed as not fitting in and they may not fulfil their potential in school and in fact may easily become disruptive.

People with an executive thinking style tend to be implementers. They like to be given guidance on how to do something and enjoy actually doing it. Executive people tend to be valued by organisations because they conform to the rules and carry out the tasks – such occupations can include police and fire services.

People with a judicial style like to evaluate rules and judge things. They prefer problems where they can analyse and evaluate ideas. Judicial people therefore like to write critiques and give opinions. According to Sternberg, therefore, the 'legislative' student would like to:

- write creative essays;

- write poems;

- write alternative endings to existing stories;

- design science projects;

- draw an original work in art.

They would dislike, however:

- writing factually based essays;

- summarising short stories;

- memorising poems;

- doing pre-packaged problems;

- remembering dates.

On the other hand, the 'judicial' student would like:

- comparing and contrasting literary characters;

- correcting other people's work;

- analysing the reason a war started;

- evaluating the strategy of a competing sports team.

They would dislike, however:

- receiving an evaluation from a teacher with no reasons given for the evaluation;

- memorising dates of historical events;

- writing a story from scratch.


## Multiple intelligence

The concept of multiple intelligence will be discussed later in this book when discussing strategies for addressing learning needs in an inclusive setting. Howard Gardner's book *Frames of Mind* and his other works (Gardner, 1983, 1985, 1991, 1999) have made a significant impact on how the abilities and the intelligences of children are perceived. Historically, verbal linguistic intelligence has been seen as being of key importance in recognising and predicting how children will perform as learners in school. To a great extent this is still the situation today. Gardner, however, argued that verbal linguistic intelligence is only one of eight intelligences. These are highlighted in Figure 4.1.

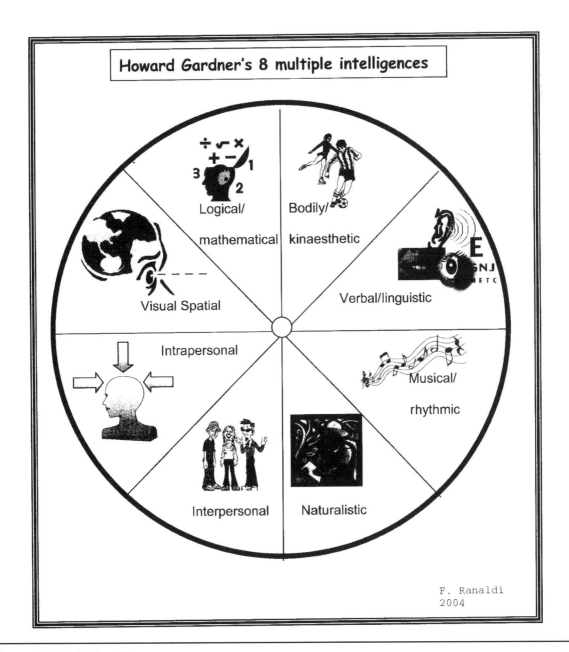

**Figure 4.1 Eight intelligences**

There have been many useful examples of how Gardner's model has been developed for assessment and for teaching all areas of the curriculum. See page 161 for a web site that illustrates this. The key point about Gardner's approach is that it recognises the diversity of children and appreciates that ability and intelligence should not be dominated by language skills. This encourages teachers to be adaptable to ensure that all intelligences are catered for in the development of class materials and in the assessment of students' work.

Many teachers have utilised the theory of multiple intelligences (MI) and have created MI classrooms where MI has a high focus in both curriculum development and assessment.

## Cognitive style

Cognitive style relates very much to information processing. Cognition relates to learning and individuals all have different ways of understanding and learning information. Riding and

Raynor (1998) suggest there are two fundamental dimensions to cognitive style – the wholist-analytic and the verbal-imagery. They define cognitive style as an 'individual's preferred and habitual approach to organising and representing information' (p8). The wholist-analytic dimension relates to whether an individual tends to organise information into wholes or parts and the verbal-imagery style relates to whether an individual is inclined to represent information during learning verbally or in the form of mental pictures.

Riding and Raynor also suggest that it is important to differentiate between 'style' and 'strategy'. They argue that cognitive style has a physiological basis and is fairly fixed for the individual. On the other hand, strategies can be developed and adapted depending on the material and the learning situation.

There have been a number of models of cognitive styles and an accompanying, sometimes confusing array of labels such as splitters and lumpers, risk-takers versus cautious, tolerant and intolerant and cognitive simplicity versus cognitive complexity. Additionally, within the wholist-analytic dimension Riding and Raynor report on a range of terms used and supportive studies. These include field dependency and independency, impulsive and reflective, converger and diverger, wholist and serialist, sequential and random and assimilators and explorers. Although these definitions are different in terms of learning and teaching they can fall into the two broad categories relating to the preferences usually associated with the two brain hemispheres, the left hemisphere being the serialist hemisphere and the right the wholist.

## Metacognition

Metacognition refers to the individual's awareness of his/her own learning. People who are skilled in metacognition will have self-knowledge in learning and be able to use that knowledge to develop comprehension and concepts across a range of learning areas. Being able to transfer learning from one source to another is a metacognitive skill which makes learning more efficient. This overlaps with learning styles because learning styles can also help learners become aware of their own learning. Learning styles therefore can foster metacognitive skills.

Learners with highly developed metacognitive skills will be able to take control over their learning. This means they will be able to direct their own learning, monitor their progress when learning a task and be able to ascertain whether or not they are on the right track. Eventually they will be able to assess their own work. Accurate and insightful self-assessment can provide an indication of the learner's metacognitive skills. Zimmerman (1989) regards self-regulation as the key to effective learning, although Nisbet and Shucksmith (1986) suggest that it can be very challenging for young children below the age of ten to develop such self-regulation. It can be argued, however, that in order to develop these skills children require practice and this practice should take place from as young an age as possible.

## Teaching style

It is recognised that teachers have different styles. There is a considerable literature on teaching style using observational and questionnaire methods of data collection. These tend to provide information on teacher types or the kind of teaching activities certain teachers are most comfortable with. For example, Grasha (1996) suggested that styles of teaching can include the following: the expert/formal authority teachers who lean towards teacher-centred classrooms in which information is presented and students receive knowledge; the personal model/expert/formal authority teachers whose approaches are teacher-centred and emphasise modelling and demonstration; the facilitator/personal model/expert teachers are student-centred and teachers design activities, social interactions, or problem-solving situations that allow students to practise the processes for applying course content; and the delegator/facilitator/expert group of teachers who place much of the learning burden on the students. Teachers provide complex tasks that require student initiative, and often group work, to complete.

Mosston and Ashworth (1990) proposed the existence of a spectrum of teaching styles that are available to teachers. These styles range from an 'autocratic' to a 'self-teaching' style. The style chosen for any lesson may vary and depends on the relationship between teacher behaviour (T), learner behaviour (L), and objectives (O). Another premise underlying the authors' work is that: *'teaching behaviour is a chain of decisions'*. Further, these decisions must be made before the lesson (pre-impact set), during the lesson (impact set) and after the lesson (post-impact set).

There is little doubt that teachers have the potential to make an impact on the students' learning. It is therefore important that teachers are aware of their style and their preferences. This is extremely important in an inclusive school where the range of students will be greater and teachers need to adapt to different abilities and learning preferences. McBeath and Mortimore (2001) highlight how research agrees that teacher effects are powerful and that there are some teacher characteristics that can increase classroom effectiveness (DfEE, 2000). While focusing on learning styles, therefore, it is important to recognise that teachers also will have preferences and that these will have an impact on the learning experience for the students in the classroom.

## Examples of models of learning styles

This section will provide an outline of some of the models that can be accessible for teachers. The Appendix of this book will provide a more comprehensive view of a range of models and the associated literature and web sites.

### Kolb's experiential learning model

David Kolb describes himself as a 'contemporary advocate of Experiential Learning'. His work in fact can be traced back to that famous dictum of Confucius around 450 BC: 'Tell me, and I will forget. Show me, and I may remember. Involve me, and I will understand.'

Kolb's twelve-item Learning Style Inventory yields four types of learners: divergers, assimilators, convergers and accommodators. His instrument and approach focus primarily on adult learners. In Kolb's model the concept of experiential learning explores the cyclical pattern of all learning from experience through reflection and conceptualising to action and on to further experience. Kolb maintains a 'Big Bibliography' which is an extensive bibliography of books and articles about experiential learning theory since 1971 (over 1,500 entries). It is updated twice a year. The latest bibliography is available from www.learningfromexperience.com.

## Honey and Mumford

Honey and Mumford defined four styles, based loosely around the four stages of David Kolb's learning cycle: activists, reflectors, theorists and pragmatists. Honey and Mumford's learning styles questionnnaire is available from www.PeterHoney.com. Honey also produces a range of user-friendly development tools, focusing on learning and behaviour.

## Gregorc's model

The Gregorc model (Gregorc, 1985) can place people along two continua: concrete–abstract and sequential–random. Individuals can therefore have a combination; for example, some can be concrete–sequential, which would indicate a strong left-hemisphere preference. Others might be abstract–random, which would indicate a strong right-hemisphere preference. Many will also have different combinations such as abstract–sequential, abstract–random, concrete–sequential, concrete–random. People will therefore possess a range of combinations from being predominantly one or two styles to a balance among all four. Gregorc's model allows teachers to identify the strengths of each type and adapt planning and teaching accordingly.

## Dunn and Dunn learning styles model

The Dunn and Dunn learning styles model (Dunn et al., 1975, 1978, 1984, 1985, 1987, 1989, 1990, 1996) identifies learning style using a Learning Styles Inventory that contains 104 items that profile the student's learning style preferences. The model focuses on five domains (environmental, emotional, sociological, physiological and psychological) and 21 elements across those domains (these are discussed further in the following chapter).

## Given's five learning systems

Given (2002) has developed a comprehensive approach to learning styles by incorporating five learning systems. These, Given suggests, are based on the brain's natural learning systems, which include emotional, social, cognitive, physical and reflective. Learning systems, Given argues, are guided by the genetic code but are subject to environmental input for their detailed patterns and responses to different learning situations. The key therefore is the interplay and it is important that teachers recognise the importance of this interplay and are able to use the natural learning systems to help children develop educationally.

Given outlines the educational implications of these learning systems by suggesting learning goals for each of them. The learning goals are:

- emotional – self-direction;
- social – self-assurance;
- cognitive – self-regulation;
- physical – self-control;
- reflective – self-assessment.

These factors provide an appropriate and useful guide for teachers. Not only will they extend the child's progress in self-learning, they will promote self-assurance and metacognitive skills.

# Implications for teaching and learning – some questions to ponder

*Is it possible to obtain a measure of fixed traits in learning and would this be a valid and reliable measure?*

It is possible to obtain a measure of fixed traits. The question is whether that measure should really determine a particular teaching approach. The term 'traits' is an unfortunate one and it does not sit well in an educational context. One of the principal foundations of education and educational opportunity is the notion that nothing is fixed. The notion that all children are capable of progressing in learning is crucial, as is the importance of viewing children in a flexible and dynamic manner. The notion of flexibility, the opportunity to progress and the perception of differences rather than difficulties are at odds with the terminology and the implications of the term 'traits'. So although many instruments will provide a 'trait' description, this should be looked upon with caution. That does not mean that any trait that is revealed in the assessment should be ignored. Rather it should be used as a guide, not a fixed prescription of what, why and how the child should be learning.

*Can this lead to a tendency to unnecessarily and narrowly label children with a particular style and can that actually be limiting in terms of the learning experience of the child?*

This is an important point and one that needs to be carefully considered by the teacher when applying learning styles to the teaching situation. Learning styles should extend learning rather than inhibit or restrict it. It is crucial, irrespective of the child's learning style, that the learning experience is enriched in as many different ways as possible.

*Is it possible to 'match' teaching styles with learning styles and is this desirable?*

It is possible and certainly in some areas of learning that are particularly challenging for the child, this should be done. It does not, however, have to be carried out in all areas of the curriculum as the child needs to gain experience in all aspects of learning and practice at using different styles. It is desirable to ensure that children/students are aware of their own learning styles so that when they are undertaking independent learning they will be able to use the self-knowledge they have in relation to their own learning.

*Should learners be encouraged to establish a degree of flexibility in the use of style?*

If this is possible then it should be encouraged. If learners can use flexibility and are able to utilise a range of styles this will enable them to deal with a wider variety of learning situations. For that reason it is probably more useful to provide opportunities that can match a wide range of learning styles, rather than providing only for one narrowly based style.

*Can learning styles instruments be used as a diagnostic aid to highlight the student's strengths and weaknesses and as a guide for planning, developing and teaching?*

Yes, definitely, this is one of the strengths of identifying learning styles. Essentially when identifying learning styles the teacher is obtaining information that will be useful for planning and teaching, and knowledge of the student's strengths and weaknesses will provide useful information for this. Identification of learning styles will therefore have diagnostic value and inform both planning and teaching.

*Can knowledge of learning style lead to enhanced metacognitive awareness, more self-awareness on the part of the student and a development in learner autonomy?*

It follows that knowledge of learning style will help the student become more aware of their individual preferences and their particular learning and study habits. This can lead to a degree of metacognitive awareness, but this needs to be developed within the teaching situation. Metacognitive awareness will not follow automatically, but students need to be trained in the use of metacognition and self-knowledge of learning will be a useful prerequisite for this.

Some of these questions were also part of the focus in the Coffield et al. study mentioned earlier in this chapter. They suggested that 'beneath the apparently unproblematic appeal of learning styles lies a host of conceptual and empirical problems'. They suggest that the learning styles field is not unified, but instead is divided into three linked areas of activity: theoretical, pedagogical and commercial. Their review identified 71 models of learning styles. They also suggested that there are few robust studies which offer, for example, reliable and valid evidence and clear implications for practice, based on empirical findings. From a scientific perspective they are very likely correct – many of the instruments may not stand up to the scrutiny based on scientific criteria of reliability and validity. However, some of those instruments that were criticised in the Coffield et al. review do claim to have a high reliability and validity. For example, the research conducted on the Dunn and Dunn model suggests that their instrument has been well evaluated. Given suggests that it has, without question, the most extensive research history with children, adolescents and adults of all learning style approaches and she cites the numerous monographs, book chapters, and hundreds of articles, and research from 112 different universities to support her claims.

## Learning styles – key points

The key points in relation to learning styles is that, firstly, every effort should be made to organise the classroom environment in a manner which can be adapted to suit a range of styles. It is also important that the teacher has an awareness of what is meant by learning styles and how to identify different styles in children, particularly aided by observation. Although there are many different instruments that can be used, teachers' observation and discussion with students while they are engaged on a task can be extremely beneficial. The different stages of the information-processing cycle can be considered in relation to how children learn and how this can be used within a learning styles structure. The experience of learning may be more important to many children than the actual finished product. At the same time it is important that all children become aware of their own learning style. This is the first, and a most important, step to achieving a degree of self-sufficiency in learning. Acknowledging learning styles therefore can help to promote skills that can extend beyond school. Knowledge of learning styles can equip all students for lifelong learning.

# Chapter 4 Overview
# Background to Learning Styles

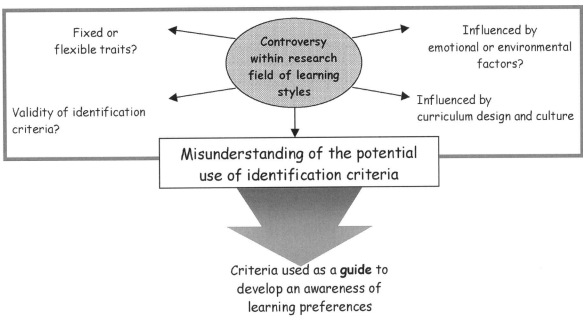

Fixed or flexible traits?

Validity of identification criteria?

Controversy within research field of learning styles

Influenced by emotional or environmental factors?

Influenced by curriculum design and culture

Misunderstanding of the potential use of identification criteria

Criteria used as a **guide** to develop an awareness of learning preferences

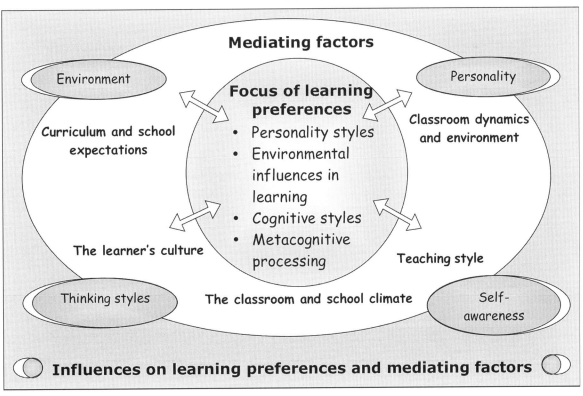

**Mediating factors**

Environment

Personality

Curriculum and school expectations

**Focus of learning preferences**
- Personality styles
- Environmental influences in learning
- Cognitive styles
- Metacognitive processing

Classroom dynamics and environment

The learner's culture

Teaching style

Thinking styles

The classroom and school climate

Self-awareness

**Influences on learning preferences and mediating factors**

# Assessment of Learning Styles

> **Outline of chapter and key points**
>
> This chapter
>
> - provides an outline of a number of different learning styles instruments;
> - discusses some issues relating to identifying learning styles;
> - provides examples from the Given and Reid Interactive Observational Style Identification;
> - gives examples of the Reid and Strnadova student and teacher instruments for identifying learning styles;
> - comments on the issues relating to linking learning styles to teaching.
>
> Key points
>
> - Critics of learning styles argue that it is impossible and misleading to identify students with a particular learning style.
> - However, for teaching and planning learning it is important to be aware of students' individual learning preferences.
> - Information obtained from observation, particularly interactive observation, can provide considerable detail to plan for learning styles.
> - Observational data can encourage students to think analytically about their learning style preferences.
> - Learning styles should not be identified in isolation, but in relation to the learning environment, the task and the curriculum.

Identification and assessment are important areas in learning styles. As the previous chapter has indicated, they can also be areas that are subject to criticism. The critics of learning styles argue that it is impossible and misleading to identify students with a particular learning style (Coffield et al., 2004). They raise doubts about whether the instruments that are currently available actually do measure learning styles and they comment on the lack of validity and reliability of many of the instruments that are currently used to identify learning styles. They do have a point. But if learning styles are seen as flexible and not as a fixed label then this criticism is less relevant. The viewpoint suggested in this book accepts that pinpointing a precise style may well be misleading and unintentionally labelling. But it is also suggested that for classroom and teaching purposes it is beneficial to use some form of identification of learning 'preferences', even if it may not be a precise or infallible measure of one's learning style. If one accepts the view that learning styles do not represent a fixed entity then equally one must accept that any instrument purporting to measure learning styles should be seen as a guide. This chapter will describe some of the well-known instruments and how these can be used to facilitate teacher understanding of the learner and the implications of this for the identification of learning preferences in the classroom.

Most of the instruments that assess learning styles are based on self-report and are essentially questionnaires. This can be problematic as the usefulness of the questionnaire relies on the individual completing the questionnaire accurately and therefore being able to identify his/her own responses to each of the items in the instrument. Some items in questionnaires can provoke a general response and the response may relate more to individual study and learning habits than any actual intrinsic learning style. For example, a popular question is whether an individual likes to listen to music while undertaking a task. This seems quite appropriate as music is known to influence attention, concentration and retention of information. But this type of question can be misleading as the question itself is fairly general and therefore the response will also have a general meaning. Additionally, questions such as these do not allow for individual changes and any variability experienced by the student in the learning environment. Some people may not have control over whether or not they listen to music while studying and other people may not even have any awareness of whether or not they actually have any preference in this particular area.

While questionnaire and self-report instruments can be useful, they only provide a guide and need to be supplemented with other means of assessment. It is advocated in this book that observation and teacher report should supplement the individual responses in learning styles questionnaires. This chapter will therefore describe an observational instrument that has been refined by the author and colleagues (Given and Reid, 1999; Reid and Strnadova, 2004). It is important to focus on the student's learning preferences in the actual learning situation and this can best be achieved through observation. Furthermore, teacher knowledge of the child's learning habits can add to the information gleaned from observation. Given and Reid have also indicated that observation can be interactive. This can be achieved by asking students about their preferences and discussing these to obtain further guidance on their individual learning preferences.

## Approaches to assessment

There are at least 100 instruments especially designed to identify individual learning styles. Many of these focus on relatively narrow aspects of learning styles such as a preference for visual, auditory, tactual or kinaesthetic input. Others are far more elaborate and focus on factors primarily associated with personality issues such as intuition, active experimentation and reflection (Gregorc, 1985; Kolb, 1984a; Lawrence, 1993; McCarthy, 1987). Some approaches attempt to identify how individuals process information in terms of cognitive style and others emphasise the body's role in learning, including laterality preferences (Hannaford, 1995, 1997).

Learning styles models have been discussed in the previous chapter but some approaches to assessment in relation to these models are discussed below.

## Cognitive style

Riding and Raynor (1998) describe cognitive style as a constraint which includes basic aspects of an individual's psychology such as feeling (affect), doing (behaviour) and knowing (cognition) and the individual's cognitive style relates to how these factors are structured and organised.

## Kolb's Learning Styles Inventory

Kolb's (1984a) Learning Styles Inventory is a derivative of Jung's psychological types combined with Piaget's emphasis on assimilation and accommodation (Piaget, 1970). Kolb's 12-item inventory yields four types of learners: divergers, assimilators, convergers and accommodators.

## Dunn and Dunn's Learning Styles Inventory

The Dunn and Dunn approach utilises the Learning Styles Inventory (Dunn et al., 1975, 1979, 1985, 1987, 1989). The inventory contains 104 items that produce a profile of learning style preferences in five domains (environmental, emotional, sociological, physiological and psychological) and 21 elements across those domains. These domains and elements include: environmental (sound, light, temperature, design); emotional (motivation, persistence, responsibility, structure); sociological (learning by self, pairs, peers, team, with an adult); physiological (perceptual preference, food and drink intake, time of day, mobility); and psychological (global or analytic preferences, impulsive and reflective).

The Learning Styles Inventory (LSI) is comprehensive and assesses elements in combination with each other. It asks students to answer the questions as if they are describing how they concentrate when studying difficult academic material. The instrument can be completed in approximately 30 to 40 minutes by elementary/primary and secondary students. After answering all the questions on the LSI answer form (the test itself), each student's answer sheet is optically read and processed individually. Each student then receives his/her own LSI individual printout – a graphic representation of the conditions in which each learns most efficiently.

## Jackson's Learning Styles Profiler (LSP) (Jackson, 2002)

According to the research conducted by Coffield et al. in the post-16 sector, this instrument appears to fare well. They suggested that the LSP is a sophisticated instrument in terms of its theory base and computerised format. Designed for use in business and education, the model describes four styles: initiator, analyst, reasoner and implementer. According to Coffield et al., the test–retest reliability of this instrument is satisfactory.

## Given's Learning Systems

Given (1998) constructed a new model of learning styles derived from some key elements of other models. This model consists of emotional learning (the need to be motivated by one's own interests), social learning (the need to belong to a compatible group), cognitive learning (the need to know what age-mates know), physical learning (the need to do and be actively involved in learning), and reflective learning (the need to experiment and explore to find what circumstances work best for new learning).

## Interactive Observational Style Identification (IOSI) (Given and Reid, 1999)

Observation by itself may not be sufficient to fully identify learning styles, but the use of a framework for collecting observational data can yield considerable information and can also verify and extend formal results from a questionnaire. A number of arguments can be put forward to support the use of observation, such as that observation is diagnostic, flexible and adaptable. It can occur in a natural setting, it is interactive and feedback is ongoing.

- **Diagnostic**: Observations provide intermittent and ongoing opportunities to analyse student responses in different learning situations.

- **Flexibility**: Interactive observations can be used across subjects, settings and interactions to surface how children learn best.

- **Adaptability**: The interactive observational framework can be adapted to different ages, classrooms and learning situations. This contextualisation allows for a holistic picture of the child's learning preferences.

- **Natural Setting**: Consistency of social behaviours, academic performance and study habits across a range of tasks can serve as an initial indicator of learning needs and preferences.

- **Interactive**: Observations can be more illuminating if some form of interaction is introduced. This can be achieved by obtaining oral responses from questions, or from the student's responses to a task. Posing questions that ask children to reflect on how they tackled a particular learning task can provide the assessor with information about children's understanding of how they learn. Engaging students in experimentation and exploration of what environmental, social and physical conditions work best for them can make the observational process highly interactive.

Metacognitive-type questions will facilitate interaction with the student. These include questions such as:

- How did you do that?

- Do you think you were successful?

- Why do you think that?

- What steps did you take to complete this?

Throughout the interaction this type of questioning can reveal information on students' learning processes and how they organise their learning. This can also provide information on students' self-perception and whether they believe the performance was due to their own skills and efforts, or to an external factor such as the teacher or others in the group or class. This latter point relates to attribution theory (Dweck and Licht, 1980) which is an important aspect of learning. It is crucial that learners are able to attribute the outcome of learning tasks to themselves when the outcome is successful and not to some external factor. This can reinforce self-belief.

Teachers can use observational data to encourage students to think analytically about their learning style preferences. Since there are no correct or incorrect style preferences, IOSI encourages students to experiment with various ways of learning and to take responsibility for determining which approaches work best for them. IOSI can serve a valuable purpose by teaching children to observe their own behaviours and performances and to take responsibility for their own learning.

Through the use of interactive observation, teachers can examine a broad range of factors that relate to the learning process. It is important to record the results systematically even though the framework is informal. Additionally the framework does not have to be completed in one period of observation. Specific aspects of the framework can be selected and the whole framework can be used over time.

---

### Interactive Observational Style Identification

---

- **Emotional**
  - Motivation
    - What topics, tasks and activities interest the child?
    - About what topics does the child speak confidently?
    - What kinds of prompting and cueing are necessary to increase motivation?
    - What types of incentives motivate the child: leadership opportunities, working with others, gold star, free time, physical activity, and so forth?
    - Does the child seem to work because of interest in learning or to please others – parents, teachers, friends?

  - Persistence
    - Does the child stick with a task until completion without breaks?
    - Are frequent breaks necessary when working on difficult tasks?
    - What is the quality of the child's work with and without breaks?

  - Responsibility
    - To what extent does the child take responsibility for his/her own learning?
    - Does the child attribute his successes and failures to self or others?
    - Does the child grasp the relationship between effort expended and results achieved?
    - Does the child conform to classroom routines or consistently respond with nonconformity?

  - Structure
    - Are the child's personal effects (desk, clothing, materials) well organised or cluttered?
    - How does the child respond to someone imposing organisational structure on him or her?
    - When provided specific, detailed guidelines for task completion, does the child faithfully follow them or work around them?

■ **Social**

■ Interaction

■ Is there a noticeable difference between the child's positive spirit and interactions when working alone, one-to-one, in a small group, or with the whole class?

■ When is the child's best work accomplished – when working alone, with one other or in a small group?

■ Does the child ask for approval or to have work checked frequently?

■ Communication

■ Is the child's language spontaneous or is prompting needed?

■ Does the child like to tell stories with considerable detail?

■ Does the child give the main events and gloss over details?

■ Does the child listen to others when they talk or is he/she constantly interrupting?

■ **Cognitive**

■ Modality preference

■ What types of instructions – written, oral, visual – does the child most easily understand?

■ Does the child respond more quickly and easily to questions about stories heard or read?

■ Does the child's oral communication include appropriate variations in pitch, intonation, and volume?

■ In his/her spare time, does the child draw, build things, write, play sports, or listen to music?

■ When working on the computer for pleasure, does the child play games, search for information, or practise academic skill development?

■ Does the child take notes, write a word to recall how it is spelled, or draw maps when giving directions?

■ Given an array of options and asked to demonstrate his/her knowledge of a topic by drawing, writing, giving an oral report, or demonstrating/acting, what would he/she choose?

■ Under what specific types of learning (reading, maths, sports, etc.) is tension evident, such as nail-biting, misbehaviour, distressed facial expressions, limited eye contact, and so forth?

■ Sequential or simultaneous learning

■ Does the child begin with step one and proceed in an orderly fashion or have difficulty following sequential information?

■ Does the child jump from one task to another and back again or stay focused on one topic?

■ Is there a logical sequence to the child's explanations or do his/her thoughts 'bounce around' from one idea to another?

■ When telling a story, does the child begin at the beginning and give a blow-by-blow sequence of events or does he/she skip around, share the highlights, or speak mostly about how the story *felt*?

■ When asked to write a report, does the child seek detailed directions or want only the topic?

■ What types of tasks are likely to be tackled with confidence?

- Impulsive versus reflective
  - Are the child's responses rapid and spontaneous or delayed and reflective?
  - Does the child return to a topic or behaviour long after others have ceased talking about it?
  - Does the child seem to consider past events before taking action?
  - Does the child respond motorially before obtaining adequate detail for the task?

- **Physical**
  - Mobility
    - Does the child move around the class frequently or fidget when seated?
    - Does the child like to stand or walk while learning something new?
    - Does the child slump or sit up when working?
    - Does the child wiggle his/her foot extensively?
    - Does the child become entangled in his/her chair when working quietly?

  - Food intake
    - Does the child snack, chew on a pencil or bite on a finger when studying?
    - Does the child seek water frequently when studying?
    - Does the child chew on his/her hair, collar or button while working?

  - Time of day
    - During which time of day is the child most alert?
    - Is there a noticeable difference between morning work completed versus afternoon work?

- **Reflection**
  - Sound
    - Under what conditions – sound or quiet – is the child relaxed but alert when learning?
    - Does the child seek out places to work that are particularly quiet?

  - Light
    - Does the child squint in 'normal' lighting?
    - Is there a tendency for the child to put his/her head down in brightly lit classrooms?
    - Does the child like to work in dimly lit areas or say that the light is too bright?

  - Temperature
    - Does the child leave on his/her coat when others seem warm?
    - Does the child appear comfortable in rooms below 68° Fahrenheit?

  - Furniture design
    - When given a choice, does the child sit on the floor, lie down, or sit in a straight chair to read?
    - When given free time, does the child choose an activity requiring formal or informal posture?

- Metacognition
  - Is the child aware of his/her learning style strengths?
  - Does the child analyse the environment in regard to his/her learning with questions such as:
    - Is the light level right for me?
    - Am I able to focus with this level of sound?
    - Is the furniture comfortable for me?
    - Am I comfortable with the temperature?
  - Does the child demonstrate internal assessment of self by asking questions such as:
    - Have I done this before?
    - How did I tackle it?
    - What did I find easy?
    - What was difficult?
    - Why did I find it easy or difficult?
    - What did I learn?
    - What do I have to do to accomplish this task?
    - How should I tackle it?
    - Should I tackle it the same way as before?

- Prediction
  - Does the child make plans and work towards goals or let things happen as they will?
  - Is the child willing to take academic risks or does he/she play it safe by responding only when called upon?
  - Does the child demonstrate enthusiasm about gaining new knowledge and skills or does he/she hesitate?
  - Is there a relationship between the child's 'misbehaviour' and difficult tasks?

- Feedback
  - How does the child respond to different types of feedback: non-verbal (smile), check mark, oral praise, a detailed explanation, pat on the shoulder, comparison of scores with previous scores earned, comparison of scores with classmates' performance, and so forth?
  - How much external prompting is needed before the child can access previous knowledge?

  (adapted from Given and Reid, 1999)

Reid and Strnadova (2004) translated the above observational framework into two instruments – one a self-report instrument aimed at students to help them identify their own learning preferences, the other focusing on the teacher's observation of the students' learning preferences.

Reid and Strnadova (2004) have piloted these instruments with both primary and secondary students and the responses from the teachers who implemented the piloting were promising, indicating that the instruments provided information that could be used to implement teaching and learning materials to cater for the range of styles in most classrooms. The instruments have been refined three times following the piloting process and are in the form of a rating scale.

Examples of both instruments are shown below.

# Pupil's Assessment of Learning Styles (PALS)©
# (Reid and Strnadova, 2004)

## Social

| 1. After school would you prefer to go home in a group rather than alone? |
| 2. Do you like playing computer games with others? |
| 3. Do you enjoy working in groups in class? |
| 4. Have you got a lot of friends? |
| 5. Do you like team games? |
| 6. Do you enjoy being with a lot of people? |
| 7. Do you like discussing topics in groups? |
| 8. Do you like doing your school work with friends/others? |
| 9. Do you enjoy spending your weekend with other people? |
| 10. Do you see yourself as a leader? |
| 11. Are you happy to share your desk with others? |

## Environmental

| 1. Is your desk/work place neat and tidy? |
| 2. Do you like quiet surroundings? |
| 3. Does sound annoy you when you are studying? |
| 4. Do you like having lots of space around you when you work? |
| 5. Do you prefer to read when sitting at a desk instead of sitting on the floor? |
| 6. Do you prefer light colours (white, yellow) in the room to darker ones (red, dark blue)? |
| 7. Do you prefer learning indoors to outdoors? |

## Emotional

1. Do you change your mind about things a lot?

2. Do you often feel sad?

3. Do you find it difficult to make decisions?

4. Do you feel confident?

5. Do you worry a lot?

6. Do you consider yourself to be reliable?

7. Do you often have headaches?

8. When you start completing your task, do you finish it?

9. Do you consider yourself as having good concentration?

## Cognitive

1. Do you enjoy doing crossword puzzles?

2. Do you remember lists?

3. Do you like to learn through reading?

4. Do you enjoy picture puzzles?

5. Does drawing help you to learn?

6. Do you like to use coloured pencils a lot?

7. Do you learn best by watching a video or television?

8. Do you enjoy experiments?

9. Do you learn best by building things?

10. Do you learn best through experiences?

11. Do you learn best by visiting places?

## Metacognitive

1. Do you like to make a plan before doing anything?

2. Do you usually think how you might improve your performance in any activity or task you have done?

3. Do you usually avoid making very quick decisions?

4. Do you usually ask a lot of people before making a judgement on something?

5. Do you find it easy to organise your ideas?

# Teacher's Observation of Learning Styles (TOLS)© (Reid and Strnadova, 2004)

## Social

### Interaction

1. Is the child's best work accomplished when working in a group?

### Communication

2. Does the child communicate easily with teachers?

3. Does the child like to tell stories with considerable detail?

4. Can the child summarise events well?

## Environmental

### Mobility

5. Does the child fidget a lot and move around the class frequently?

### Time of day

6. Is the child most alert in the morning?

7. Is the child most alert in the afternoon?

## Emotional

### Persistence

8.  Does the child stick with a task until completion without breaks?

9.  Does the child require only a little teacher direction in doing the task?

### Responsibility

10.  Does the child take responsibility for his/her own learning?

11.  Does the child attribute his/her successes and failures to self?

12.  Does the child work independently?

### Emotions

13.  Does the child appear happy and relaxed in class?

## Cognitive

### Modality preference

14.  Does the child readily understand written types of instructions?

15.  Does the child readily understand oral types of instructions?

16.  Does the child readily understand visual types of instructions?

17.  When you are giving instructions, the child (mark 1–4):
     ■ asks for a lot more information
     ■ draws maps (for example, mind maps)
     ■ takes notes

### Sequential or simultaneous learning

18.  Does the child begin with step one and proceed in an orderly fashion rather than randomly jump from one step to another?

19.  Are the child's responses delayed and reflective rather than rapid and spontaneous?

### Tasks

20.  Is there a relationship between the child's 'misbehaviour' and difficult tasks?

| Metacognitive |
| --- |

**Prediction**

21. Does the child make plans and work towards goals rather than let things happen as they will?

22. Does the child demonstrate enthusiasm about gaining new knowledge and skills rather than hesitate?

**Feedback**

23. How does the child respond to different types of feedback (1 = low/negative response, 4 = high/positive response):
   ■ non-verbal (smile)
   ■ check mark
   ■ oral praise
   ■ a detailed explanation

**Structure**

24. Are the child's personal effects (desk, clothing, materials) well organised?

25. Does the child respond negatively to someone imposing organisational structure on him/her with resistance?

26. When provided specific, detailed guidelines for task completion, does the child faithfully follow them?

27. Does the child seem to consider past events before taking action?

The information received from these two instruments should provide pointers for the identification of the learning preferences of the student and for the development of teaching approaches and can also help with classroom organisation and group work, particularly in deciding the composition of groups.

## Linking assessment with practice

The responses from a learning styles instrument should have practical implications for the teacher as well as for the learner. If there are 30 learners in a class then the teacher will have difficulty in catering for 30 different styles. It is almost certain, however, that there will not be 30 different styles and there will be some types of styles that the teacher can combine. For example, learners who are visual are often kinaesthetic and may also be global – meaning that they prefer to see the whole before the individual pieces of information – and prefer working in groups. This would mean that learners in this category will be able to access similar materials and respond effectively to similar teaching and learning approaches.

It can be suggested that students can become more independent in their learning as a result of knowing their strengths and weaknesses. Students therefore can develop more effective learning strategies which they can use outside the classroom.

Coffield et al. cite the views of Alexander (2000), who distinguishes between 'teaching' and 'pedagogy'; and they argue that the learning styles literature is principally concerned with teaching rather than pedagogy. They take this as evidence that teachers need to be cautious about using the learning styles literature as a guide to classroom practice and argue that there is a need to be highly selective, as some approaches are more relevant than others.

One of the key questions that needs to be considered by the teacher when planning on using learning styles is 'what is it being used for?' In other words, learning styles should not be identified in isolation but in relation to the learning environment, the task and the curriculum. Using a learning context for learning styles can be more meaningful and ensure that the approaches used and the materials developed are developed not only for the student but in relation to the task the student is to embark on. This means it is important that every subject teacher has knowledge of learning styles as well as the student's individual profile. Although all learners' styles should be accommodated in every subject, there may be some variability and restriction depending on the subject. The important point is that the identification of learning styles needs to be linked to teaching plans, teaching methods and teaching strategies. It is for that reason that the framework described earlier in this chapter (Given and Reid, 1999) was developed. This framework allows for flexibility and can be used to accommodate to the learning and teaching needs of all students in all subjects of the curriculum.

The learning process is integral to, and affected by, the interaction between teaching and learning styles. It is important that this should be seen as a high priority even though the research to support this may not be abundant. Coffield (2005) argues that one needs to be careful about attempting to match teaching and learning styles because of the conflicting research evidence. It is important, as Coffield also claims, that students and staff in schools and colleges reflect on their own learning and that of others. This should lead to learners being taught to set explicit, challenging goals and to identify strategies to reach these goals. This is one of the reasons why the identification of learning styles is important as it can help students become more aware of their own learning and be able to reflect more effectively on the actual learning strategies and the learning environment.

This chapter has provided a summary and suggestions for identifying learning styles. Many teachers opt for simpler and less complex visual, auditory and kinaesthetic approaches. These are certainly easier to identify and easier to implement. It is important, however, not to unduly restrict a learner by focusing too much on one or other modality. These and other approaches to identifying learning styles will be discussed in the following chapter on learning and teaching and in Part 4 of this book, which looks at effective learning. The key point is that learning styles should be identified for a purpose and set against a learning context. For that reason some other instruments and methods of identification are discussed in Part 4.

# Chapter 5 Overview
# Assessment of Learning Styles

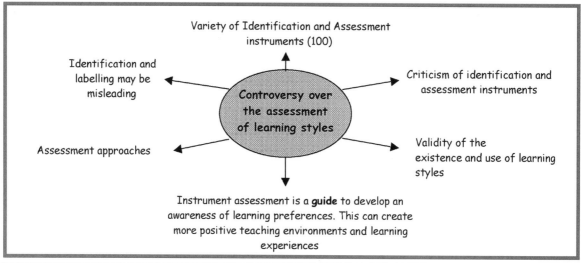

Variety of Identification and Assessment instruments (100)

Identification and labelling may be misleading

Controversy over the assessment of learning styles

Criticism of identification and assessment instruments

Assessment approaches

Validity of the existence and use of learning styles

Instrument assessment is a **guide** to develop an awareness of learning preferences. This can create more positive teaching environments and learning experiences

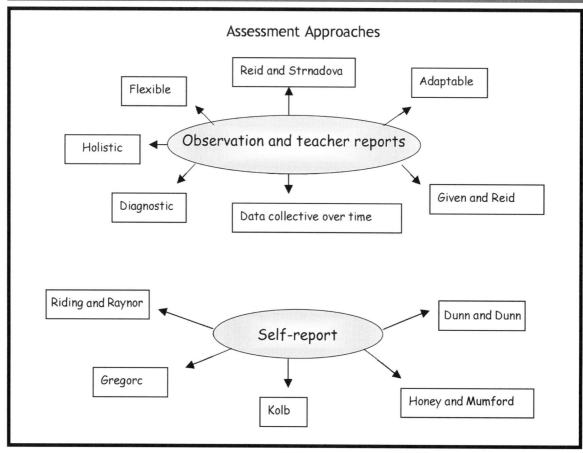

## Assessment Approaches

Flexible

Reid and Strnadova

Adaptable

Holistic

Observation and teacher reports

Diagnostic

Data collective over time

Given and Reid

Riding and Raynor

Self-report

Dunn and Dunn

Gregorc

Kolb

Honey and Mumford

# Learning Styles – Learning and Teaching

**Outline of chapter and key points**

This chapter

- discusses and provides examples of learning styles approaches in the classroom;
- considers learning and teaching within the context of the curriculum and the inclusive educational environment.

Key points

- The traditions in the school, the expectations and the principles that govern curriculum development can all provide barriers to the successful implementation of learning styles.
- Classroom discourse and classroom dynamics can be influential and can have an influential effect on pupils' learning.
- Encouraging students to choose the types of tasks, questions or modes of working can be an enabling strategy that can increase learning opportunities.
- It is difficult for the teacher to ensure that all children will have their learning styles matched to particular teaching approaches, but when developing materials, tasks and other teaching resources every attempt should be made to consider the diverse styles that will be evident in the classroom.
- The classroom can be a strategic learning environment and this is as much about the nature of the teaching and learning as about the opportunities to access resources.
- The social and emotional needs of students are paramount and these should not be overlooked because of any preoccupation with matching learning to teaching.
- The range of students' learning styles can be incorporated into the planning of learning in every school subject.
- Student self-knowledge is important and students could be made aware of the advantages and disadvantages of different styles.
- It is important, however, not to pigeonhole students by their learning styles as this can be unnecessarily restrictive.

# The learning context

In some situations the learning and the teaching context can provide considerable challenges for teachers. The conventions in the school and the expectations and the principles that govern curriculum development can all provide barriers to the successful implementation of learning styles. For example, it is more difficult for learning styles to be considered within a traditional exam-focused formal school environment than one that is influenced by more flexible criteria. An interesting example of this is the 'Learning without Limits' project in the UK (Hart et al., 2004). The project was established in 1999 at the University of Cambridge School of Education with the aim of studying the distinctive features of teachers and classrooms free from ability labelling. Quite apart from the arguments concerning ability testing, the key message of the project was that ability-orientated teaching is restrictive and unfair. The project team argued that there are educational, social and moral arguments to justify abandoning ability labelling. Additionally, attribution theory suggests that 'locus of control' is an important determinant of motivation to learn and is important for a successful learning experience. This means that if students feel they have control over their learning and can attribute success or failure to factors they have control over, then they will be motivated to work to improve their learning and achievements. If, however, they attribute success or failure to factors beyond their control they will lose the sense of power to influence this. The effects of ability labelling can therefore be potentially damaging and restricting for many learners. Ability labelling is usually associated with traditional classrooms, which may be a learning context that is not conducive to the implementation of students' learning styles. Willes (1983) showed that traditional styles of classroom discourse tended to encourage brevity and passivity on the part of pupils. This indicates that classroom discourse and classroom dynamics can be influential and can have an impact on pupils' learning. The project highlighted a number of detailed case studies. One such study was described as a thinking skills classroom and the features of this were:

- every child has something to offer;

- it is important that no child misses out on significant learning opportunities;

- every child is entitled to the same learning experiences – framed to suit their needs;

- enjoyment and interest have an important place in children's learning;

- the learning process should involve planning, adjusting, reflecting, targeting and enabling;

- it is important to encourage children to make links – 'nothing happens in isolation' (Hart et al., p71);

- the need to encourage children to think for themselves;

- 'knowing your pupils' is the key to success;

- the need to be open-minded about the children in the class and see them as individuals;

- the need to consider children's different learning styles;

- learning styles tie in with getting the best out of children;

- learning styles helped in looking at overall planning;

- the need to transcend limits and expand opportunities;

- flexible grouping and flexible tasks;

- social learning is a fundamental foundation for academic learning;

- children need to have a sense of ownership over the classroom environment;

- there needs to be a supportive emotional learning environment;

- information on children's learning styles can be obtained from noticing and responding, from 'watching the class and see what and how they learn' (Hart et al., p126).

(adapted from Hart et al., 2004)

The above research project found that learning styles were an influential factor in establishing 'learning without limits'. One of the main factors in relation to this was factors relating to student choice. One teacher-participant found that encouraging students to choose the types of tasks, questions or modes of working was the most enabling strategy and increased challenge and learning opportunities. This was enhanced by allowing students to discuss their learning styles and preferences openly in class and by encouraging tolerance and understanding of other styles.

Another important factor in the above project is that the nine teacher members of the team worked in diverse settings as regards – buildings, resources, traditions, ethos and curricular objectives – yet they were all able to lift the limits on learning by adopting some of the approaches outlined above. There was a 'view expressed that reconsideration of the needs of individual learners is exciting to see, both in schools and across all learning institutions and this is essential for learning without limits to take place' (p237).

## Matching teaching and learning styles?

It is a commonly held view that one of the purposes of identifying learning styles is to match teaching methods to learning styles. In an inclusive classroom, however, this may not be realistic and can place considerable pressure on teachers. There are two points of importance to be considered. These are:

- the importance of ensuring that classroom activities and materials are sufficient to meet a **range** of styles;

- assistance should be given to students to ensure that they have an awareness of their own learning style.

The key point is that when planning and developing materials, tasks and other teaching resources the potentially diverse range of styles that will be evident in the classroom needs to be considered.

## Steps in planning learning style-based instruction

Keefe (1991) suggests the following procedure when planning for learning styles teaching:

1. Diagnose individual learning styles.

2. Profile class or group tendencies and preferences.

3. Determine significant group strengths and weaknesses.

4. Examine subject content for areas that may create problems for learners with weak skills.

5. Analyse students' prior achievement scores and other products (curriculum-referenced tests, skill tests, portfolios, etc.) for patterns of weakness that may reflect cognitive skill deficiencies.

6. Augment (remediating weak cognitive skills).

7. Assess current teaching methods to determine whether they are adequate or require more flexibility.

8. Modify the learning environment and develop personalised learning experiences.

It can be useful to identify students' learning profiles. The examples below suggest categories such as social, environmental, emotional/metacognitive and cognitive.

## Social

Students with a social learning style will have preferences for working with others. This means that students with this style will need to seek out others when about to tackle some challenging work, as they will find they need to talk about the task to others and in fact can be inspired by others.

## Environmental

The type of learning environment selected (preferred) by students can make a difference to the outcome of their learning. It is usually best for such students to try to study in an environment in which they feel comfortable. For some students this can be the most important aspect.

## Emotional/metacognitive

This relates to how aware students are of their own learning preferences. It also relates to awareness of their emotions. These factors can be important for learning and for the student developing autonomy in learning.

## Cognitive

This relates to how students actually process information and think. Cognition means thinking and it is important to establish students' most effective thinking style. Knowing this can help students learn more efficiently.

## The role of the teacher

Teacher perceptions, teaching style and willingness to engage in learning styles and help students to take charge of their learning are basic to the success of learning styles teaching.

Given and Reid (1999) indicated that the following teaching principles can serve as a guide for developing learning styles teaching:

- Acknowledge children's unique learning style strengths.

- Help children understand how to use learning strengths for academic success.

- Develop children's appreciation for the unique learning styles of self and others.

- Encourage students to develop secondary and tertiary strengths.

- Design structured lessons for high student interest and content value.

- Prepare well-designed and well-planned materials for students.

- Teach students how to reflect on their own learning.

- Empower children to take charge of their own learning.

- Teach children to keep records of their own progress.

- Challenge students to improve on their personal best.

- Monitor student performance and growth.

- Make adjustments as needed to ensure achievement by every child.

The UK learning skills report (Coffield et al., 2004), although critical of the concept of learning styles, appreciated that some of the approaches currently advocated by those who promote learning styles can actually make for effective learning. They referred particularly to the potential of learning styles to help the learner achieve 'deep' and strategic learning and to act as an agent for broader change. They suggest that open-ended dialogue between tutor and student can begin to identify forms of support such as courses on study skills and should lead to discussion of the curriculum and of assessment. The authors of the report felt that this may in turn encourage tutors to discuss among themselves how they can improve students' approaches to learning. It was felt that this could have an impact on the ethos of the institution and act as a springboard for an exploration of pedagogy and cultural change. They concluded that 'learning styles can be a catalyst for individual, organisational or even systemic change'(Coffield et al., p60).

## Teaching and assessing learning styles

A multi-sensory framework that involves visual, auditory, kinaesthetic and tactile learning styles is a good starting point as it will incorporate some of the students' preferences. Nevertheless, it is important the students are assessed and present work in a range of modalities. Therefore activities involving drama and art, poetry and creative writing should be seen as just as relevant to the assessment process as more formal written assignments. This is particularly important as there is a strong view (West, 1997) that a great number of children with special educational needs often have skills in the creative areas and can be demotivated by constant failure in the more traditional subjects assessed through traditional means.

As indicated earlier in this book, there are a number of instruments that can help to identify students' learning styles and preferences. However, in the classroom context it can be reasonable for the teacher to identify these preferences through the process of observation and the teacher's knowledge of the student while engaged in the teaching process.

Although observation can provide more information on the child's learning habits, it is also a good idea to ask students themselves to articulate how they are engaging in a task and what kind of learning environment they prefer for the task. Children are often able to say whether they prefer music, low light, making lists or starting a task with a drawing. Obtaining this information can help the teacher present new information initially at least in the child's preferred style of learning as this will maintain motivation. One of the most demotivating factors in learning is repeated failure, or having to expend considerable effort for little return. Many children who have difficulties in learning can experience these feelings of failure. Very often this can occur in the early years, after having been in school for only a short time. If knowledge of learning styles and of the student's personal learning preferences can prevent failure, then it is essential that every teacher is aware of this and has the opportunity to investigate and develop appropriate materials for the range of learning styles that can be found in classrooms.

# Self-esteem

The other factor that can help to prevent failure is that of raising self-esteem. It is important for all to recognise that the social and emotional needs of students are paramount and these should not be overlooked because of any preoccupation with matching learning to teaching. This should of course be attempted, but the self-esteem needs of the students must also be high on the agenda. One of the benefits of focusing on self-esteem is that programmes or strategies of this nature will benefit everyone. Additionally, self-esteem strategies can be integrated into a programme of work that can also acknowledge the student's learning style.

## How can self-esteem be acknowledged within the teaching and learning process?

Some points to consider include the following:

- Ensure that all the objectives that are set are achievable and that students recognise this.

- Make the student feel important and that his/her personal contribution to the class is important.

- Use the student's name all the time when speaking to him/her.

- Point out positive aspects of the student's work first when assessing it.

- Allow students to make choices and praise them for the choice they have made.

- Display students' work.

- When a student asks a question, try to indicate the positive points about the question, but not in a patronising way.

- Try to vary the assessment strategies used in the class so that all students will be able at some point to use their preferred styles.

- Spend time discussing a difficulty with the students and try to show how the experiences can be used positively.

- Encourage students to experiment with their learning and to take risks – always praise the outcomes by indicating the positive factors.

- Ensure that the particular working groups that students are allocated to in class are constructive for them. It is worthwhile spending some time ensuring the group dynamics are right.

- Try to take an interest in the student as a person – discuss his/her interests and their life outside school.

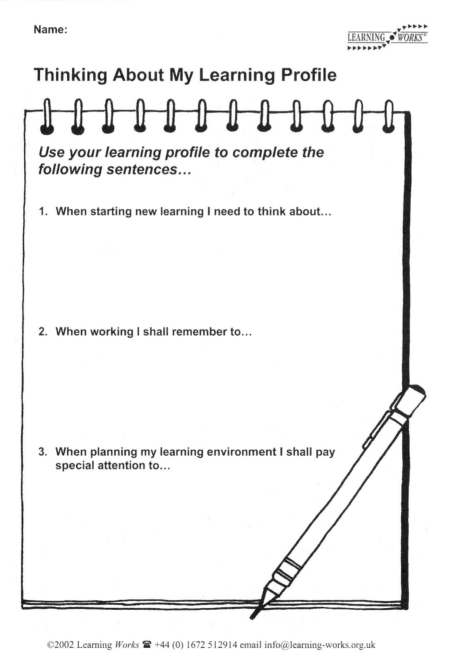

**Name:**

LEARNING ● WORKS®

## Thinking About My Learning Profile

*Use your learning profile to complete the following sentences...*

1. When starting new learning I need to think about...

2. When working I shall remember to...

3. When planning my learning environment I shall pay special attention to...

©2002 Learning *Works* ☎ +44 (0) 1672 512914 email info@learning-works.org.uk

**Figure 6.1 Thinking about my learning profile**

- Use programmes such as circle time and other self-esteem programmes that involve developing social skills and collaborative activities.

- Try to integrate team-building exercises into the daily work of the class.

Cooke et al. (2002) provide an excellent range of activities that focus on learning styles and these can also be used for developing self-esteem. For example, the extract in Figure 6.1 contains three simple questions but these can lead into important discussions and can give the student a sense of importance.

## Strategies

In the UK the National Strategy (DfES, 2002) comments on the use of learning styles for different subject areas of the curriculum. Many of these can be seen in a generic way as the general principles of these learning styles strategies and can transfer across to other subject areas. For example, in history the strategy guidelines suggest the following can be useful in relation to using learning styles in the classroom:

- talk;

- drama;

- drawing;

- the voice;

- hearing texts read;

- role play;

- bodily movement;

- feeling;

- moving things around;

- facial expression;

- props;

- reflecting;

- conversations;

- collaborating;

- mapping;

- imagining;

- observing;

- visualising content.

## Science

One of the key features about science is that much of the work takes place in a collaborative manner. Experiments may be undertaken jointly and the learners often have a degree of responsibility in carrying out the experiments. This can lend itself to interpersonal learning and provides the opportunities for students to engage in activities that will enhance knowledge about themselves and others. Working with others in a collaborative learning environment can be a powerful social activity.

## Modern languages

Modern languages can be challenging for many students. Yet it is an area where learning styles can be used in every aspect of the teaching process. The students who are most at risk of failing in modern languages are those who do not have an auditory learning style. Those with an auditory style can more easily tune in to the particular characteristics of the language while on the other hand students who are visual and kinaesthetic will need additional considerations when material is being presented to them. Certainly illustrations and video enable concepts to be introduced using the target language without using English. Similarly, pictures used as flash-cards will help students recall language at a visual prompt. It is also helpful to develop association with the students so that they can associate the picture with the word.

It is important to recognise that the students at risk of failure in the languages classroom would usually have an informal learning style and may have a visual/kinaesthetic learning preference. Some general principles and strategies that might be useful are:

- Provide large print hand-outs.

- Provide a visual structure that can allow students to compose their own notes.

- Consider using a range of mnemonic devices to help students remember and retrieve information that is difficult to study and recall.

- Encourage students to invent and practise their own designed mnemonic strategies.

- Guide students to find mnemonics that work best for them.

- Develop units of work that involve short tasks and indicate how the new information connects with the previous task.

- Provide opportunities for the students to discover the connections themselves by providing prompts.

- Ensure the learning steps are small.

- Teach in a multi-sensory way – this helps to ensure that irrespective of the students' preferences they will at least be able to find one of the approaches suitable.

- Provide an emphasis on kinaesthetic–tactile learning as this is useful for many learners with difficulties in language learning and they usually learn more effectively in this way.

According to Schneider and Crombie (2003), activities for the language classroom that provide kinaesthetic–tactile learning opportunities include:

- explicit modelling and practising of how to verbalise language concepts while acting them out as persons or sorting colour- and/or shape-coded cards on desks or on the floor;

- using different types of fabric and other materials to help with the association and memorisation of different concepts through touch (e.g. soft fabric for voiced letter-sound and hard fabric/material for unvoiced letter-sound).

Schneider and Crombie also suggest some general principles teachers can follow to ensure that all learners are included. These include the following:

- Using multi-sensory techniques: Multi-sensory techniques actively involve students in using their stronger channels of learning to bring on the weaker ones. The motto is 'Hear it, see it, say it, write it, act it out', and make learning as active as possible.

- Structure: Restructuring the language material so that the more complex topic builds on the easier using discovery techniques for the students to see how the new information fits in with the previous.

- Overlearning: Make sure the student receives opportunities for overlearning and practice through providing a variety of activities.

- Metacognition: Make language learning a 'discovery learning' process in which students turn into 'language detectives', finding out about the structures and uniqueness of the new language, why certain expressions are used the way they are and how the students can self-correct and monitor their own reading and writing. This makes all students independent learners.

- Motivation: Engage students by activating their personal strengths and interests and by giving them individual space (e.g. permission to walk around at the back of the room if they become overactive).

It can be suggested that kinaesthetic–tactile/hands-on involvement in learning is vital to maximise the probabilities of success for memorising and retrieving information in the languages classroom.

## Physical education

Physical education can be a subject that is very much geared to kinaesthetic learners. Yet students will still need to engage in some writing and this can be problematic for some. Instructions for sport and games may also be in written form or provided in auditory form. For kinaesthetic students this can also be problematic. They will learn more effectively if they are provided with demonstration and will learn from the experience of participating in the activity.

Students with a kinaesthetic style are usually good at observing and visualising. This means they can use their observational skills first to learn how to do the activity and if any writing is to be involved this can be done at a later stage, by which time the student will have a good grasp of what is involved in the activity. This will make the writing process easier for them. Activities and the key points in a game or sport can be shown to the students as a visual sequence of actions. The key points therefore, instead of being written, can be demonstrated by visuals.

## Mathematics

Mathematics is a subject that involves both auditory and visual/spatial abilities. Not all students have preferences in both. It is important therefore that a range of strategies is used to put across the mathematical concepts that are to be learnt.

The DfES (2002) suggested that when teaching geometrical reasoning, teachers should encourage students to use their hands to estimate and 'feel' angles; or move their whole bodies to experience rotation. Such physical activities help conceptual understanding and can make subject terminology more accessible and more easily understood.

## English

English is without doubt a subject that can accommodate to a range of learning styles. Activities such as role play and drama can involve a range of learning styles. Experiential learning can be very suitable for learners who have difficulty in learning through the auditory mode or those who have difficulty in reading text, and many areas of the English curriculum can be taught in this way.

It has been suggested that asking students to say their opening sentence aloud to a partner before they start to write can encourage them to hear their writer's voice. Writing frames can also be used to provide students with a structure and cues for written work The web site http://www.warwick.ac.uk/staff/D.J.Wray/Ideas/frames.html contains examples of this strategy. Writing frames can also be provided in a visual form so that the pictures provide the cues rather than the key words (see Chapter 2).

## Teaching style

One of the issues relating to meeting the needs of diverse groups of learners in the classroom is the teacher's personal experiences and of course the teacher's own personal learning style. Some learners will feel more comfortable with certain teachers. It is important therefore that teachers are aware of their own learning style and aware of the kind of teaching situations they may feel less comfortable with.

The academic culture is a key element in how a teacher may relate to his/her own style. In some schools the academic culture is predominantly auditory, particularly in traditional schools. However, more schools are now appreciating the importance of learning styles and are requesting staff development in this area. Having carried out a number of staff development days to all staff in schools – both primary and secondary – I find the question most frequently asked is 'How can I cater for the full range and diversity of learning styles in my class?' This is a reasonable question and the answer to this question lies in fact in one word that was used by the questioner – **diversity**. Any lesson, no matter what one is teaching, needs to cater for diversity. Teaching approaches and materials need to be diverse and by ensuring this, one will automatically cater for a range of styles. It is in fact good teaching to ensure that you are providing a number of examples to highlight a point. By doing that you may illustrate a point by getting the students to act out or dramatise the material that is being learnt or provide visual examples.

# Principles to motivate all learning styles

- **Balance** – try to ensure that teaching and planning incorporate a range of styles and that there are activities that can accommodate to visual, auditory, kinaesthetic and tactile learners as well as having areas of the room to accommodate different environmental preferences.

- **Planning** – teachers need to engage in learning styles at the planning stage. It is important that at that stage information about the learners is obtained. The observational framework in the previous chapter can be useful for this.

- **Collaboration** – learning styles should be seen as a whole-school issue and responsibility. To successfully implement learning styles in the classroom, environmental considerations need to be acknowledged and this may need the co-operation of other teachers and in particular the school management. Implementing learning styles can be more successful when the whole school is involved and preferably the whole school district or education authority.

- **Differentiation** – differentiation is about good teaching and planning and if the task and the curriculum are effectively differentiated to take account of the task, the input, output and the resources that are to be used, then it is likely that all learning styles will be catered for in some way.

- **Learner awareness** – it is worthwhile spending time with the learner so that he/she will be aware of their own learning preferences. It will be useful to help them understand that there are advantages and disadvantages to every style.

# Advantages and disadvantages of each of the styles

## Auditory learner

### Advantages

If you are an auditory learner you will benefit from listening to talks and lectures. You will also absorb a lot of information from radio programmes. You will very likely have skills in sequencing and organising information and have a methodical approach to many aspects of your life. You may remember information by using a checklist. You can often be considered to be a reliable and independent worker.

### Disadvantages

There is a possibility you may have to complete one task before embarking on another. There is also a possibility that you focus on small bits of information and do not obtain a holistic and broad picture of something you are working on. You may also prefer to work on your own rather than work in groups.

## Visual learner

*Advantages*

You will be good at visualising events and information and may be able to use your imagination to some advantage. You can use visual strategies for remembering information. You may also get considerable pleasure from learning involving visual and creative skills. You may be able to see the whole picture when discussing or working on a problem or task.

*Disadvantages*

You may need more time to complete tasks. You can be more interested in the appearance of something than its actual value – that may be a disadvantage in some situations, though not in all. You may not spend enough time on or pay attention to specific detail.

## Kinaesthetic learner

*Advantages*

You will enjoy active learning and this is useful for assembling and making products. You will be able to demonstrate to others how to do something. You will likely be able to enjoy the actual experience of learning.

*Disadvantages*

You may miss some instructions or information if it is presented orally. You may find it difficult to concentrate on a lengthy written task while seated. You may not pay attention to detail, especially if it is in written form.

## Social/emotional learners

*Advantages*

You will enjoy working with others or in teams. You will also try to engage others to be involved in a task and therefore you may be quite motivating. You will enjoy working in groups and will have a prime concern for the wellbeing of colleagues and friends. You will thrive on discussion and this can be very stimulating for you.

*Disadvantages*

You may become too dependent on assistance from others. You may have difficulty in structuring a task if you are completely on your own. You may be influenced to a great extent by your feelings and these might affect your judgement.

## Metacognitive learner

### Advantages

You will be good at reflecting and problem-solving. You will be able to use previous learning efficiently when learning new information. You will need time to consider all possibilities and this can be appreciated by others and they may seek out and trust your advice.

### Disadvantages

Your style of learning may be frustrating to others if you are working in a group. You may appear pedantic and take a long time to carry out a task because of this.

# Comment

One of the principal points to appreciate in learning styles is that all styles can be effective. However, the actual task demands can make one type of style less effective than another. For example, if the student has to locate detailed information from a library using index cards or computer referencing then an auditory style may be more effective and the visual learner may have to use a visual strategy to do this. But when it comes to locating books from the shelf the visual learner may be able to locate the title of the book from the visual appearance of the book faster than the auditory learner can from the book reference number. At the same time it is important not to pigeonhole students by their learning styles as this an be unnecessarily restrictive. It is important not to think that a certain type of learner is incapable of learning using another mode. It is for that reason that teaching and planning of learning should involve a range of learning experiences that can reinforce learning and ensure that all styles are accommodated in the mainstream classroom.

# Chapter 6 Overview
# Learning Styles – Learning and Teaching

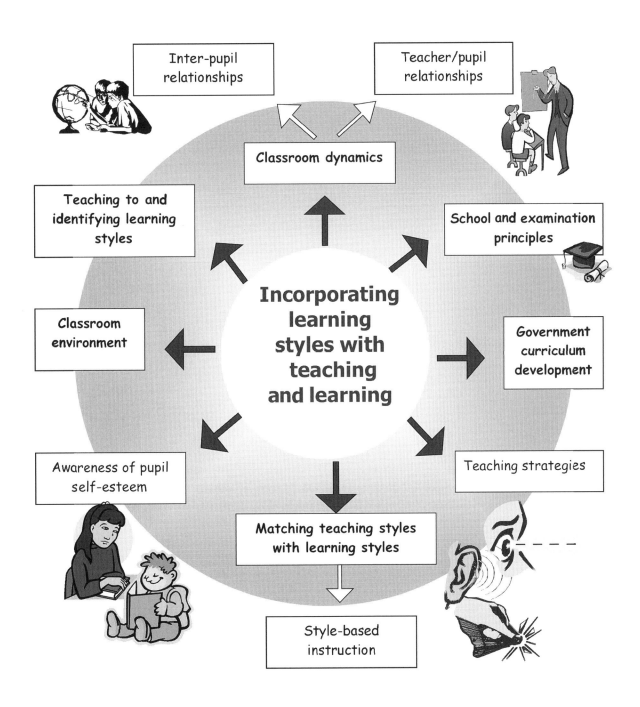

Inter-pupil relationships

Teacher/pupil relationships

Classroom dynamics

Teaching to and identifying learning styles

School and examination principles

**Incorporating learning styles with teaching and learning**

Classroom environment

Government curriculum development

Awareness of pupil self-esteem

Teaching strategies

Matching teaching styles with learning styles

Style-based instruction

ART 3

# INCLUSION

HAPTER 7

# The Inclusive School – Characteristics and Challenges

**Outline of chapter and key points**

This chapter

■ examines the concept and the role of inclusion in education;

■ discusses the characteristics of inclusion;

■ explains why inclusion can be challenging for teachers, children and parents.

Key points

■ Inclusion does not happen – it is a process.

■ School culture and collaboration are essential for inclusion.

■ Differentiation is important for successful inclusion and learning styles can be an integral component of differentiation.

■ Inclusion can highlight a potential conflict between meeting the needs of individuals and meeting the needs of all.

■ In an inclusive school learning styles need to be embraced by management as well as by the individual teachers.

There are a number of important and unresolved issues relating to inclusive schooling. While most agree that the concept and the values associated with inclusion are of considerable merit, the actual practicalities of inclusion can be challenging. Additionally, the inclusion debate centres on social and political issues as well as those of direct educational relevance to teachers. One of the areas of contention surrounds the most desirable provision and practices for those children identified as having special educational needs. Riddell (2002) highlights that there has always been a desire to separate out children with special educational needs. Even those who attend mainstream school usually have special classes or attend a dedicated on-site unit. But as Riddell points out, this has been accompanied by a desire to achieve social equality and the knowledge that children with special needs will require additional resources. There are inherent conflicts contained in these desires, between providing additional resources and at the same time considering the budgetary obligations of the school; and between promoting social equality by providing inclusive schools at the cost of individual freedom of choice. One way round these conflicts is to ensure that the quality of inclusive schools is high and that the needs of all learners are met.

In the UK a set of materials known as the Index for Inclusion (Booth et al., 2000) was developed to support the process of inclusion in schools. The Index was distributed to 26,000 primary, secondary and special schools in a government funded initiative. Three key areas are described in detail in the Index. These relate to inclusive cultures, inclusive policies and inclusive practices. These three areas have considerable relevance for successful inclusion, but also for learning styles as each can have a role to play in helping to meet individual needs and recognising individual preferences for learning within an inclusive educational setting.

Inclusion does not happen – it is a process. Inclusion develops over time and the success of inclusion depends on the preparation and the foundations that have been put in place. Tomlinson (1997) defines inclusion as matching the resources we have to the learning styles and educational needs of the students. This definition recognises the need of student-centred approaches if inclusion is to be successful. At the same time, while the aim of inclusion is to cater for all, it is important that the individual needs of children, particularly those children with 'additional' and special educational needs, are not overlooked. Florian (2005) suggests that 'inclusive education is not a denial of individual difference, but an accommodation of it within the structures and processes that are available to all learners' (p96). While children with special needs might benefit from an inclusive setting, they will require some additional considerations in terms of the structures and processes of meeting their educational, social and emotional needs. Acknowledgement of learning styles and learning preferences can help all children adapt to an inclusive setting.

## Inclusive cultures

It can be argued that this is the most influential aspect of inclusion. If the culture and the climate are not inclusion-friendly then the outcome, irrespective of policies or indeed practices, may not be successful. The Index for Inclusion (Booth et al., 2000) suggests that inclusive cultures need to be created and are about building communities and establishing inclusive values. Booth et al. suggest that 'it is about creating a secure, accepting, collaborating, stimulating community in which everyone is valued … it is concerned with developing inclusive values … [and these] guide decisions about policies and moment to moment practice so that learning of all is supported through a continuous process of school development' (p45).

Some of the key points include:

- the need for cultures to be created;

- the need for acceptance of all individual differences;

- the need to ensure effective communication and collaboration;

- the need for recognition that policies and practices develop over time and an acknowledgement that this development is influential in the formation of inclusive cultures.

Jordan (2001) tackled the challenges of creating inclusive cultures head-on when investigating the problems faced by Travellers' children in state education. She argued that some of the problems evident in this group were also shared by other vulnerable learners. These problems included lack of cultural respect and support, irrelevant curriculum and inappropriate forms of curriculum delivery, low expectations, harassment, bullying and self-exclusion. The Travelling community historically has an oral tradition with oral storytelling rather than print being the principal means of transmitting knowledge. Clearly this has implications for learning styles and indeed the literacy tradition established in most schools may explain why many Travellers' children are disaffected with schooling. Jordan reports on a number of projects supported by the European Federation for the Education of Children of Occupational Travellers (EFECOT, 1999) that have been implemented. Interestingly, looking through the list of projects it is easy to recognise that learning styles could be introduced and utilised throughout all of these projects. For example, the projects included pre-school work packs, guidance on early reading skills, culturally appropriate literacy packs and teacher training packs to develop in-school approaches and curriculum development. But as Jordan reports, despite this 'good level of support Travellers' children still question the relevance of school education beyond the primary stages (ages 5–12) and even when enrolled at school have high levels of absences'. She also claims that this is not due to institutional racism as there is evidence of self-exclusion from Traveller-only schools 'that are run by very positively disposed professionals … in France, Spain, Belgium, USA and the Netherlands' (Jordan, 2001, p131). These findings raise a number of questions. But clearly school for this group of learners is neither exciting nor relevant. Yet when interviewing teachers and school management on learning styles for this book, I was struck by the learning culture of the school and excitement generated by the learners when engaged in activities using their learning preferences. Additionally, as the following chapters show, the abundance of learning games and activities that often accompany learning styles programmes can themselves generate excitement in learning. This example of Travellers' children is a good case in point of where learning styles could have allowed this group to benefit fully from a totally inclusive educational culture and climate.

## What is an inclusive culture?

The Index for Inclusion referred to above suggests the indicators of an inclusive culture are that:

- everyone is made welcome;
- students help each other;
- staff collaborate with each other;
- staff and students treat one another with respect;
- there is a partnership between staff and parents (carers);
- all local communities are involved in the school.

These points are extremely relevant to the notion of learning styles. In fact it can be argued that by acknowledging the individual learning preferences of students, all the above points will in some way be acknowledged.

## Everyone is made welcome

Essentially this means that all individuals and all individual differences are to be acknowledged. There is much to be said in support of the notion that children know if they are not welcome and similarly will feel comfortable when they are made welcome.

*Criteria for the welcoming school*

- notice on entrance door saying 'welcome' in different languages
- children's work on walls
- recognition of different cultures on wall displays
- recognition of different abilities on wall displays
- photographs of children
- emphasis on activities
- focus on school's achievements
- emphasis on school's role in the community
- indication that parents are made welcome
- sitting room for parents
- opportunities for parents to see teachers/management without appointment – for example, a drop-in centre

## Collaborative learning

One of the key reasons for acknowledging learning styles is to promote a situation where collaborative learning is possible and effective. It is accepted that some children, and indeed adults, will find it difficult to work together. That is because their respective learning styles can be conflicting. It is possible to use learning styles to promote effective group work, ensuring that the children in the group will work harmoniously. But even a conscientious student can become disruptive if the group composition is not conducive to his/her learning style. This can also be applied to staff development when teachers are working in groups. During workshops I usually ascertain the learning style of the participants and allocate groups according to their learning styles. There are many different learning styles approaches that can be used to highlight this. One particularly relevant approach is Psycho-Geometrics™ (Dellinger, 1989) (www.drsusan.net/). This allocates shapes to each style – for example, the following characteristics would be noted for each shape:

- square – precise, attention to detail, requires facts, focused;
- rectangle – flexible, needs support, transitional;
- circle – conciliatory, good at listening, good interaction skills;

- triangle – directional, goal-oriented, leader, good at making decisions;

- squiggle – erratic, creative, individual, not much awareness of time.

It can be seen from the characteristics noted above that some shapes would be in conflict with others and if a group was composed of participants with the same shape preference, disruption might well occur. For example, a group that comprises all 'triangles' might argue and jostle for control, squiggles might get out of control, squares would try to control you and make demands, and circles might not be focused enough and spend too much time discussing the task. Similarly, triangles or indeed squares might get rather frustrated at the antics and ideas of squiggles and a circle might get rather anxious if in a group of squares or triangles because they might think the group is not reflecting on the task sufficiently.

Groups with some balance of styles may work more effectively. Squares and squiggles can often work well together as each can complement the other. Depending on the individuals, triangles can be complemented by circles, as can squares. This is just one example but it highlights the importance of planning and preparation in allocating children into groups for class activities.

According to Dellinger (www.drsusan.net), 'circles have so many friends, triangles always get the best "deals", squares will not tolerate sloppy work, squiggles are so embarrassing, and rectangles can't remember anything'. This should be borne in mind when allocating groups.

## Staff collaborate with each other

The above formula can be applied to staff, and some staff will need a different kind of support and consultation pattern from others. Circles will want long drawn out discussions while triangles may just want a quick decision to be made. Staff helping each other is as much about recognising the individual styles of learning, working and interacting as about the function of the role of a teacher.

## Staff and students treat one another with respect/There is a partnership between staff and parents (carers)

These two aspects can go together. They are essential for successful inclusion and do rely to a great extent on personalities and styles as much as the opportunity for collaboration. It is important to recognise this and to take this into account when allocating groups and activities.

## All local communities are involved in the school

This is a crucial aspect of inclusion and indeed can be at the very heart of an inclusive system. Inclusion is not only about what happens in the classroom, but the extent that society as a whole participates in the education and the inclusion of young people. It is important that all parts of the community are involved. But the key point is that involvement needs to be constructive and seen to be useful by all parties. Clearly, planning can ensure that this happens, but knowledge of learning styles can also ensure that the input from communities will have an impact on the individual children in the school. If a presentation is being given from someone from the community, the class teacher can assist in the preparation by ensuring that the visitor is aware of the children's learning styles and the need to include activities that can accommodate to all styles.

## Inclusive policies and practices

Learning styles for many teachers relate directly to the classroom and the teaching and learning activities that take place in the classroom. This involves planning on the part of the teacher. But in order for learning styles to have a full impact in an inclusive setting it needs to be taken into account in policy.

Norwich et al. (2001) sound some caution in relation to the implementation of the Index for Inclusion discussed earlier. They argue that the language of the Index might be seen to question the assumption of specialisation and special educational needs. Their concern centres on the strong focus on the social model evident in the Index. This, they suggest, raises conflicting dichotomies such as inclusive versus special needs education, and a social versus a medical model. One needs to examine how these two sets of dichotomies can be maintained within an inclusive system. Practical examples of this can be found in some special schools that have developed constructive and interactive links with mainstream schools. There is a good example of this reported by Reid (2005b) who interviewed a head teacher (Lannen, 2002, personal interview) of a special school, the Red Rose School in England, which is a dedicated short-term provision for children with specific learning difficulties. Most of the children admitted to the school have failed in the mainstream setting and have, not surprisingly, low levels of self-esteem, as well as low attainment. But within this specialised resource, which operates a clear focus on learning styles, the children progress well and most of them are eventually readmitted to mainstream schools or further education. It can be argued that within this dedicated 'special provision' the principles of inclusion are operating. All children within this environment have an entitlement to the full curriculum and to have their social, emotional and educational needs met. Moreover, Lannen reported that because they all have acquired self-knowledge and have been able to use their learning style in all subjects, they have developed skills that can be used for independent learning.

Mittler (2000) implies that successful inclusion policies need to promote inclusion whenever possible. This involves practical support, staff development and partnerships. Learning styles can have a role to play in each of these factors and staff development is central to developing the system of support that can ensure successful inclusion. It is at this point that learning styles can be introduced. When learning styles are introduced, however, it is important to ensure that staff do not see them as fixed characteristics. This is the inherent danger in closely adhering to learning styles. Learning styles need to be seen as a guide to intervention, not a prescription.

Rose (1998), in discussing curriculum delivery in an inclusive setting, argues that there is a tendency to oversupport the student and this he maintains can become 'a tool for isolation' (p34). He suggests that it is preferable if students, particularly students with special needs, do not become too dependent on additional support in the mainstream school. Additionally, such support usually relates to curriculum content and often the person providing the additional support may not have the same detailed knowledge of the curriculum content as the mainstream teacher. There is therefore an argument for suggesting that support should not be in the form of curriculum content but rather in the learning process. The effect and the impact of such support can easily be transferred to other learning situations and this can promote independence in learning.

# Individuals with Disabilities Education Act (IDEA)

In the US the Individuals with Disabilities Education Act (IDEA) (US Government, 2001) contains requirements that can in theory strengthen progress towards inclusive practices. This legislation requires school districts to place students in the Least Restrictive Environment (LRE). Therefore if the Individual Educational Plan (IEP) of a student with a disability can be implemented satisfactorily with the provision of supplementary aids and services in the regular classroom, that placement will be seen as the LRE for that student. Nevertheless, in practice, this still presents considerable challenges and tensions for teachers. These are discussed below.

# Challenges and tensions

## Challenges

There are a number of tensions that need to be resolved in relation to inclusion. These tensions arise because of the conflicting needs that often occur in providing all students with equitable learning opportunities. This can include conflict in school management and the equitable use of resources. This presents a challenge to educators – teachers, management, administrators and support staff. Although the challenges associated with inclusion have often been coupled with those relating to special needs, it can be argued that all students offer a uniqueness and present a range of individual variations in learning and personality. Norwich et al. (2001) make an interesting comparison between individual needs and common needs. Individual needs arise from characteristics that are unique to the child but different from all others, while common needs arise from characteristics shared by all. It can be suggested that learning styles can cater for both individual needs and common needs. While a number of individual needs can be equated to the term 'special needs', it can be suggested that the characteristics are more relevant than the label (Reid, 2004). Children with 'special needs' have both 'individual needs' and 'common needs'. In this context common needs would mean emotional development, achievement and learning opportunities.

The figure of 20 per cent is usually suggested in relation to the incidence of special needs, which would imply that individual considerations need to be given to this group, and the remaining 80 per cent of children will have 'common' needs. This means that by tailoring learning styles to meet both 'individual needs' and 'common needs' the needs of all children will be met. Nevertheless, this takes considerable preparation and understanding of the individual characteristics of the students in the class.

Giorcelli (1995, 1999) suggests that the controversy surrounding the inclusion movement is due to the lack of preparedness of teachers in mainstream schools for students with high support needs and the adoption of inclusion practices without a rigorous focus on educational outcomes.

These are just a few of the challenges that can be associated with inclusion but the key point is that the individual needs of all children need to be met and this proposition is in itself both daunting and challenging to teachers. Differentiation, which is referred to in several chapters of this book, is one means of dealing with this, but even differentiation requires careful and skilled planning and implementation. Learning styles can be an integral component of differentiation and can assist teachers to deal with the challenges of inclusion.

## Tensions

Wearmouth et al. (2002) recognise the challenges noted above and suggest that the current educational context is one that attempts to reconcile the principles of individuality, distinctiveness and diversity with inclusion and equal opportunities. There are inherent conflicts in this. There is a universal drive to raise the learning and achievement standards of all pupils through whole-class and whole-group teaching and standardised assessment. Yet there is a statutory obligation to acknowledge the principle of inclusion for all pupils. This can contribute to tensions and anxieties on the part of teachers. While inclusion can be seen as a desirable outcome in terms of equity, it can also be seen as a threat and a potential conflict between meeting the needs of individuals and meeting the needs of all.

## Provision

It can be suggested that one of the contradictions of inclusion arises because it is equated with the shift from segregated provision to inclusive provision. For some this is the cornerstone of inclusion and needs to be achieved at all costs. Unfortunately, often the costs are high. Many parents still support segregated provision of children with special educational needs (Lannen et al., 2004). Nevertheless, it is still important, whether a child is in a segregated or inclusive educational environment, that learning preferences and learning styles are included in the planning and delivery of the curriculum.

Diniz (2002) argues that inclusion must be perceived by the profession as much more than the move from segregation to integration. Inclusion needs to incorporate social and ethnic groups who may be at a social, economic and educational disadvantage. In this context learning styles (and teaching style) can also have a role to play. There is evidence of cultural influence in both learning and teaching. Guild (2001) quotes Gardner (1991), who indicates that we 'are as much creatures of our culture as we are creatures of our brain' (Guild, 2001, p38). She also cites Bennett (1986), who claims that 'culture shapes learning style, students who share a teacher's ethnic background will be favored in class' (Guild, 2001, p96). Bennett also suggests that if classroom expectations are limited by the teacher's own cultural orientations, then this can have a restricting effect on learners from a different cultural orientation. At the same time the individual differences need to be acknowledged as not all people within a culture will have the same characteristics.

Guild suggests that there is consistent agreement that variations among individuals are as great as commonalties within a cultural group. Although culture does affect learning styles, according to Guild distinct learning style patterns don't fit a specific cultural group. This point is supported by research from Dunn (1997), who claims that 'researchers have clearly established that there is no single or dual learning style for the members of any cultural, national, racial, or religious group' (Dunn, 1997, pp74–5).

Nevertheless, it is important to acknowledge the influence and the impact of cultural orientation when identifying, developing and providing inclusive education for school and for society (Landon, 2001; Posch, 2004). Landon suggests that 'if the norms operating within a school and through the social and learning opportunities which it provides are predicated on the assumption of fixed power relations … on the myth of cultural and linguistic homogeneity, then those who operate outside that power structure and whose cultures and languages are different will effectively be excluded from the life of the school' (p182). Similarly, Posch (2004) highlighted the diversity of cultural orientations over a relatively small area of South America.

## The practice

One of the key aspects to ensuring that inclusion is effective in terms of practice is to ensure the tasks that are set for students and the objectives that have to be met actually match the students' needs and, importantly, that the students have the means to achieve these needs and outcomes. Often children fail because of unrealistic objectives and learning outcomes. That is because objectives are not set for individual needs, but for curriculum or examination practicalities and are geared more to the community of learners than to individuals. Simpson and Ure (1993) describe some statements on matching tasks to pupils' needs. They found that teachers who effectively manage the match:

- share the management of learning with pupils;

- promote the belief that things can improve by demonstrating that agreed learning strategies work;

- use a wide range of sources of information;

- give and receive continuous feedback in terms of how pupils are getting on.

These statements confirm the need to incorporate students' perspectives into the practical development of inclusive practices. Each of these statements can also be consistent with the need to acknowledge learning styles in the classroom.

Sharing the management of learning with pupils is a good example of this. In developing and teaching to learning styles one is essentially working collaboratively with the students and helping to manage their learning. Moreover, this implies that a student is encouraged to be reflective in relation to his/her own learning. Learning styles can help students become more self-aware and more reflective in terms of their own skills and strategies for learning.

The General Statement on Inclusion (QCA, 2000) on 'providing effective learning opportunities for all pupils' sets out three 'key principles for inclusion'. These are:

- setting suitable learning challenges;

- responding to pupils' diverse learning needs;

- overcoming potential barriers to learning and assessment for individuals and groups of pupils.

While all these statements are consistent with learning styles, the statement 'responding to pupils' diverse learning needs' in particular can have a direct impact on learning styles. This is one of the challenges in inclusion and the needs of students can be wide ranging. Learning styles can provide one example of how these needs can be met. A comment often made by teachers is that they do not have the expertise nor the experience to deal with the wide range of needs found among students in most schools. This is often the case, but the use of learning styles, as can be seen in Chapter 2, can make the task of meeting the diverse needs less challenging.

Wedell (2000) proposes a broader concept of understanding and dealing with diverse needs. He proposes an 'interactive' model of difficulties in learning. In this model the barriers to pupils' learning arise as a result of the interaction between the characteristics of the child and what is offered through the pedagogy and supporting resources. This implies that one has to have knowledge of the child's characteristics as well as of the means to support that child. It is at this stage that learning styles needs to be considered.

Furthermore, Wearmouth (2000) argues that a number of factors make schools as institutions incapable of responding to the learning needs of all pupils:

- regimentation of pupils;

- lack of individuality and personal recognition;

- chronological age grouping;

- inappropriate model of child-as-learner;

- within-school power relationships;

- authoritarianism.

If this is the case, developing inclusive practices will be extremely challenging. The above factors could pave the way for alienation and exclusion rather then inclusion. It can be argued therefore that as school traditions stand at present, meeting the diverse needs of all will be challenging and may result in the needs of some students being overlooked. The strength of a learning styles model is that it incorporates all and can, by doing this, extend school effectiveness.

## Some features of inclusion using learning styles

- **Diversity** – the student population is becoming less and less homogeneous and it is important therefore that the learning styles of all students are recognised.

- **Collaboration** – teachers planning together can create more effective problem-solving strategies and can help to create a learning styles approach that can be used in the whole school. Learning styles in an inclusive school are not the responsibility of one teacher.

- **Flexibility** – schools and teachers need to be adaptable to the wide range of student needs and learning styles.

■ **Assessment** – it is important that students are able to demonstrate competence in a variety of ways and not be restricted to a formal written examination.

■ **Integrity** – it is also important that the students' needs are placed before policy implementation and administrative obligations.

■ **Ambition** – the needs of all should be catered for, including the most able. All students need to be set goals that will extend them and their horizons and goals.

■ **Harmony** – all organisations work and function more effectively when there is harmony. Inclusion can generate some tension and conflict and it is important that this does not prevent collaboration nor affect the school climate and ethos. These factors are essential for a smooth-running, efficient and effective school.

Learning styles should be implemented from a top-down as well as a bottom-up perspective. This means that they need to be embraced by the school management as well as the individual teachers in the school. This point will be developed in the next chapter.

## Chapter 7 Overview

# The Inclusive School – Characteristics and Challenges

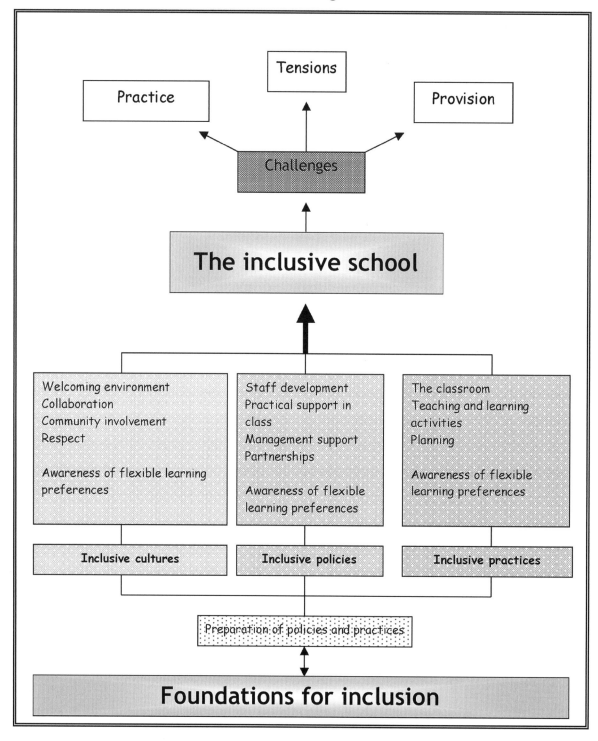

# Learning Styles in the Inclusive Context

**Outline of chapter and key points**

This chapter

- discusses some of the key issues that need to be considered when developing and implementing learning styles approaches in classrooms;
- provides frameworks and suggestions for implementing learning styles;
- considers approaches to differentiation, combined with learning styles, as a means of dealing with the diversity of students evident in most classrooms.

Key points

- Learning styles are more effective when implemented on a whole-school basis.
- Planning for learning styles should consider the curriculum, the planning and contextualising of learning objectives and the development of metacognitive awareness and self-assessment.
- Differentiation is a process and needs to be carried out taking all factors into account, including the task, the content, the presentation and the outcome.

Learning styles are integral to the process of learning and this must be considered when curriculum development is taking place. But if learning styles are to be effectively implemented the whole learning environment needs to be immersed in learning styles, students need to be aware of the importance of different styles of learning and how they can utilise their preferences for the different tasks they have to complete. The context therefore for learning styles is not only confined to the classroom, but rather should involve the whole school.

How does one start to consider how to implement learning styles in the classroom and the school? There is no exact formula for this. The approaches used will vary from school to school. There are, however, some guiding principles that should be considered. These are discussed below in a six-step framework. This begins with the identification of need and progresses to the goal of self-assessment. One of the objectives of implementing learning styles is to develop the learner's self knowledge. If students can utilise self-assessment this would indicate that they have developed insights into their own learning. The steps indicated below provide a framework for leading to the ultimate goal of self-assessment. Knowledge of their learning styles can help students reach that goal.

**Step 1  Identification of need**

| Learner's needs | Learner's current performances | Curriculum objectives |
|---|---|---|
| e.g. To develop reading fluency | Difficulty reading irregular words | To read, with understanding, informational texts |

This is important as it relates to assessment, but not in a negative way; rather the implication is that one is attempting to identify the learner's needs and to match those to the learner's current performances and the anticipated curriculum outcomes. Needs can be identified through administrating a learning styles questionnaire, literacy assessment, if appropriate, and an observational framework (see Chapter 5). Some of the questions that can arise when identifying needs include:

- What do learners want to achieve? What are they motivated to accomplish? These points should be decided through discussion with learners.

- Why do they want to do this? This can help to obtain their perception of the task.

- How will it help them achieve further knowledge and skills? What type of foundations can be laid for further learning?

- What is preventing them meeting their needs? This can be related to cognitive, environmental and curriculum factors.

**Step 2  Reframing curriculum objectives**

| Current objective | Revised objective | Steps to achieving objectives |
|---|---|---|
| e.g. Reading with understanding informational-type texts | Identify informational texts | Locating informational texts in library |

This is important because if expectations and targets are too ambitious, the student will be demotivated from the outset. This can lead to low self-expectations and to learned helplessness. Some questions that can be asked in relation to reframing curriculum objectives include:

- What are the curriculum objectives?

- Why have these been selected?

- What previous knowledge/competencies do the learners need in order to achieve these curriculum objectives?

■ Are the objectives realistic given the above?

■ In what way are learners prepared to meet these objectives?

■ What barriers can be anticipated in meeting these objectives?

### Step 3  Planning the learning process

| Learner's needs | Objectives | Strategies |
|---|---|---|
| e.g. To read fluently | Develop sight vocabulary | Word banks, wall displays, tapes |

This step incorporates the different aspects within the learning process. This would involve identification of needs, developing objectives and devising strategies. It is important that at this stage the potential range of learning styles is taken into account. This would ensure that all children will have opportunities to use their preferences. This involves more than incorporating visual, auditory, kinaesthetic and tactile elements, but also involves ensuring there is a variety of learning environments available for students. This would include provision for a quiet corner as well as the opportunities for group work. The learning process should relate to the curriculum objectives and the learner's needs.

### Step 4  Contextualising learning for individual learners

| Preferred strategies | How these can be implemented | How outcomes can be measured |
|---|---|---|
| e.g. Need to administer learning styles questionnaire/observation | This will involve discussion with students | An opportunity should be provided for students to demonstrate competence using their preferred learning style |

It is at this stage, when the curriculum objectives have been set and the learning process defined, that there will be an opportunity to develop individual programmes based on individual learning preferences. It is also possible at this stage to match the strategies and the preferences that are to be used with how performances are to be measured. It can be challenging to develop a range of assessment measures, but this is necessary if there is to be a match between the learning preferences used and the means and criteria envisaged to measure outcome. For example, if the student is a kinaesthetic learner, drama can be used in achieving the curriculum objectives. But the assessment should also have a kinaesthetic element (Eadon, 2004).

Yet even if a student's learning style is clearly 'kinaesthetic' there may still be an argument for making the assessment written, thus ensuring that the student's writing skills are not neglected. Coffield (2005) argues that 'one danger of an unthinking use of learning styles is that the teacher views a student as being a certain type of learner, incapable of learning via another mode; worse still, learners may end up with a limited view of themselves' (p28). Although this is open to debate, the all-round development of the learner's skills should be considered although it is often useful to introduce a new or challenging topic using the learner's preferred mode.

## Step 5  Developing metacognitive awareness

| Learner's awareness of learning styles | Awareness of task objectives | Awareness of how task can be achieved |
|---|---|---|
| This can be achieved through discussion with the learner | The learner can be questioned orally to ensure he/she is aware of the learning objectives | The learner needs to demonstrate orally or in a plan how the task is to be carried out |

The ultimate goal of 'learning' is to help the learner become an efficient and effective learner. Metacognitive awareness is part of this. 'Metacognition' means thinking about thinking and metacognitive awareness relates to the students' awareness of the task, how the task can be achieved, students' current levels of readiness for the task and how they may acquire the resources and the skills to achieve the task. This thinking process develops into self-knowledge and this type of knowledge can help students become efficient learners. It can help learners become aware of how they need to approach the task and the steps to complete the task.

Flavell, one of the earlier pioneers of this approach (Flavell, 1976; Flavell and Wellman, 1977), suggested four broad and slightly overlapping categories of the cognitive process involved in learning. These are reported in Nisbet and Shucksmith (1986) and include:

- Basic operations of cognition – the process of cueing or association by which an object is recognised.

- The knowledge component – this helps in the development of concepts and converts the material to meaningful information to aid comprehension.

- Strategies – these are conscious behaviours and relate to 'knowing how to' rather than just 'knowing'.

- Metacognition – that is knowing about knowing – that relates to the individual's knowledge and awareness of memory and the existing knowledge that is relevant to the new information. The student at this stage would be able to transfer learning with some ease.

It is important therefore to consider the learning process and the need for the student to aspire to the metacognitive level. Knowledge and the utilisation of learning styles will increase self-awareness and this can help the student achieve the desired metacognitive awareness.

## Step 6  Self-assessment

| Self-direction | Self-monitoring | Self-assessment |
|---|---|---|
| Being able to direct their own learning without supervision | Being able to monitor progress and decide if they are on the right track | Being able to give an indication that the task has been completed correctly, and what they may do to change what they did to make future learning easier |

Self-assessment is the ultimate goal of the learning process. It would mean that students have control and an understanding over their learning. It would also mean that they have the ability to identify how they may be going in the wrong direction in a particular task and importantly, how they might put that right. In reading, self-correction is seen as being a desirable skill and indicates that the reader has control over text and is obtaining meaning from the text. Similarly, self-assessment would indicate learners are in control of the task and have an understanding of what the task is about. This has implications not only for the specific task learners are currently working on, but also for future learning.

Nisbet and Shucksmith (1986) suggest that much of the responsibility for this lies in the way children are trained for learning. Often they are not trained in this way. Nisbet and Shucksmith suggest that such training should include:

- 'teaching not only subject or task-specific skills, but also the "subordinate" skills or strategies that encourage children to integrate skills in a way that will encourage transfer from task to task and

- training children to develop an awareness of how they may control and monitor the learning process' (p76).

These ideas are as relevant today as they were in 1986. They also represent a means by which curriculum materials and teaching and learning can be made more meaningful for all.

## Developing appropriate curricula

The term 'appropriate curricula' is often used in planning for learning. To achieve appropriate curricula, however, it is necessary to focus on appropriate learning. This can be very clear when one looks at the work of David Lazear in relation to teaching for multiple intelligences. Lazear (1994, 1999) has developed a multiple intelligence menu that can help all students irrespective of their style access the curriculum. An example of how such a menu might look is shown below.

Appropriate learning

| Verbal/Linguistic | Visual-Spatial | Logical-Mathematical | Bodily-Kinaesthetic |
|---|---|---|---|
| Essays | Puzzles | Higher-order reasoning | Dramatisation |
| Word search | Exercises in logic | Outlining | Dance |
| Memory games | Deductive reasoning | Pattern games | Mimes |
| Drama | Calculations | Logic exercises | Games |
| Speeches | Logical analysis | Deductive reasoning | Demonstrations |
| Debates | Copying designs | Calculation process | Invention projects |
| Diary writing | Developing designs | Logical analysis and critique | |

(adapted from Lazear, 1994)

This example emphasises the two components of learning – the content and the process. Both are necessary but it is important that the need for knowledge – the content – does not restrict the process. It has been indicated elsewhere in this book that learning styles can be a catalyst for effective and efficient learning habits. Using the multiple intelligence principles in lesson preparation and assessment can pave the way for the use of learning styles and for the development of creative and problem solving thinkers.

Setley (1995) reports that many children who have difficulty performing in school appear to show three patterns in their learning – they learn inefficiently, inconsistently and incompletely. She argues this can have consequences for brain development and the strengthening of neural pathways. Because learning has not been strengthened and consolidated, the pathways will be fragile and the information will be understood and retained only in a fragmented manner. Setley provides a model of learning that takes the potential obstacles to learning into account. She describes four stages of learning from exposure to mastery. The exposure stage is when a new idea or concept is being introduced. At this stage some confusion can arise as the learner attempts to assimilate the new information. The guided learning stage implies that the learner still requires support and has not yet reached a level of competence in the skill, or in the understanding of the material. The next stage is the independent stage and here the learner gains competence and confidence in his/her abilities. The final stage, the mastery stage, comes after extensive practice. This occurs when learners can undertake a skill or task almost without thinking. Arriving at this stage, however, is very difficult for many students. Yet in order to utilise learning and skills for new learning, and to become a more effective, consistent and complete learner, it is necessary to develop mastery, or at least achieve independent learning. The key point in relation to this chapter is that students, particularly those with difficulties, are more likely to progress through these stages if their learning styles are acknowledged in the planning and development of materials and in the learning environment. This implies that planning for learning styles needs to be proactive and for that reason it is best carried out as a whole-school task, involving all staff.

## Classroom management

The challenge for teachers is not so much identifying learning styles, but in developing the mechanisms that can accommodate to the wide range of learning styles in the classroom situation. This can be achieved through differentiation and pre-planning. But first the actual 'learning needs' and the learning styles of the individuals in the class need to be identified. A framework for classroom management of learning styles should therefore incorporate the following:

1. Identify the overall assessment strategy – for example, self-report, observation.

2. Administer the instrument to identify individual learning styles.

3. Develop individual programmes for the children in the class in accordance with the curriculum content and objectives.

4. Plan how the content can be differentiated in terms of presentation.

5. Identify resources that will be necessary to support the range of styles.

6. Identify and plan the classroom environment that can incorporate the range of styles.

7. Identify the assessment strategies that are to be used to measure competence and success.

8. Provide some guidance to students that can help them develop self-direction and self-assessment.

Teachers, however, are very aware of the barriers that might prevent learning styles being implemented in the classroom. A discussion with some teachers on that particular issue provided interesting results. One teacher suggested that many staff in the school are reluctant to utilise learning styles because of the time implications in planning and revisiting their own practices. This teacher felt that teachers should be encouraged to observe other teachers and share good practice and knowledge of the children and their individual differences. She felt, however, that the quantity of work that teachers need to get through is definitely an obstacle to implementing learning styles in the classroom.

Another teacher who teaches in a secondary school in the UK suggested that the main barriers to implementing learning styles at his school were:

■ lack of belief and interest in new ideas;

■ teachers teaching the way they have been taught;

■ not enough time to develop new ideas (this is a major issue);

■ staff turnover – hence lack of continuity within departments.

This teacher, however, has implemented programmes on study skills and learning styles and suggests the way forward is to provide:

■ more in-class development of learning styles and study skills;

■ teachers being given the appropriate training;

■ acknowledgement and support from the school management;

■ students to be provided with a range of learning opportunities, such as group work, friendship groups, pair working and individual working.

The key question, according to this teacher, is how these aspects can be managed and the school management be fully supportive and involved. The important yardstick, he suggests, is that the teachers and the pupils must be able to see the benefits of working this way. It is important that learning styles are used in all subjects and need to be incorporated within lessons. In this particular school all senior students have study skills seminars that incorporate learning styles and the emphasis is on helping students assume responsibility for their own learning (personal correspondence, 2005).

In Canada a teacher responding to the same questions, who teaches in Vancouver, suggested that one of the difficulties is the lack of precision and clarity in IEPs (Individual Educational Plans). She indicated that very often IEPs for students that have been tested and found to have learning differences will indicate 'adaptations', use visual aids, monitor progress and other general 'teaching routines' that good teachers do all the time with children, regardless of whether they have an IEP or not. The challenges, however, of dealing with classes of over 20 are considerable. She indicated:

> I have problems with statements like 'provide additional help' and explain instructions individually. I can identify two barriers to implementing learning styles to cater for the diversity in most classrooms. How do I manage it when I have twenty other students to work with (and that's a small class) and how do I manage it without the child being completely embarrassed?
>
> I try to overcome these barriers by asking different students to volunteer to read passages from the text and have a student paired with sympathetic and understanding peers who will explain the instructions to the student.
>
> We do have a 'skills center' at our school where students get extra help individually or in small groups and it seems to work very well. (Breslin, 2005, personal correspondence)

Another view from Canada (Green, 2005) suggested that teachers have difficulty in allocating time to create resources that teach to a specific learning style. 'In training, however, teachers are increasingly taught about Multiple Intelligences and learning styles. The main barrier is putting that information into practice.' This teacher suggested that 'they need to have thematic units with exercises adapted to different learning styles to help with ideas and suggestions'. This is a valuable point and one that is picked up in the following chapter. There are also a number of other barriers such as:

- the tendency for students to be grouped according to ability;
- the criteria for assessment;
- the diversity found in most classrooms.

These are crucial points and emphasise the need for the implementation of learning styles to be carried out, not only by the class teacher but with the collaboration of the school management. One way of dealing with the diversity in classrooms and integrating learning styles in daily practice is through effective differentiation. This can be very challenging and is discussed below.

## Differentiation, individual programmes and short- and long-term targets

There is a great deal written about differentiation. Much of it focuses on the aspect of differentiation by content and this is an essential aspect for successful differentiation. Differentiation, however, encompasses more than that. It needs to focus on how the materials are presented as well as the assessment process. That is the process, the product and the outcome. Visser (1993) suggests that 'differentiation is the process whereby teachers meet the need for progress through the curriculum by selecting appropriate teaching methods to match an individual child's learning strategies within a group situation'. Successful differentiation therefore hinges on knowledge of the child's needs. This requires careful planning and assessment in order to identify the type of differentiation that would be most suited for that child. Planning needs to consider:

- individual differences;

- learning styles;

- building on past achievement;

- challenges for further achievement;

- opportunities for success.

The key points here are that differentiation needs to be individualised for a particular child. That does not mean that the content has to be differentiated for every child. The important point is that differentiation should make the child's learning experience more meaningful. This will depend on how the material is presented and how the outcomes are to be measured. It is important that the student perceives the task as achievable. This might mean changing classroom management style. This is not always easy. It is also important for teachers to review how successful they have been with a particular aspect of differentiation. For that reason it is best to embark on any planned programme of differentiation in groups. This will help in the evaluation and also make classroom and environmental modifications more possible because everyone will be involved.

## Differentiating instruction

Tomlinson (1999) suggests that at its most basic level, differentiating instruction means 'shaking up' what goes on in the classroom so that students have multiple options for taking in information, making sense of ideas and expressing what they learn. This means that a range of learning possibilities are available for students to acquire the content, understand the information and meet the learning objectives.

Tomlinson suggests that differentiated instruction should be:

- proactive;

- more qualitative than quantitative;

- aimed at offering multiple approaches to content, process, and product;

- student-centred;

- incorporating a blend of whole-class, group, and individual instruction.

The factors that need to be considered in relation to this are the:

- curriculum;

- learner;

- task;

- presentation;

- outcome.

Tomlinson indicates that although it is challenging for teachers to adapt to the range of needs, it is important to recognise that in differentiated classrooms, learners will bring many commonalities to school, but that they also bring the essential differences that make them individuals. It is this blend between meeting the individual needs and allowing the common elements to surface that comes from classroom experience and knowledge of the learners – their learning preferences and their learning needs.

There are many models relating to what differentiation is and how it can be effectively developed for all learners. One of the most well known is differentiation in the following three ways:

- by task – setting different tasks for students of different abilities;

- by outcome – setting open-ended tasks that can allow students to respond in a variety of ways;

- by support – by providing additional help.

The website www.greenfield.durham.sch.uk/differentiation.htm provides a useful range of terms and explanations relating to the dimensions of differentiation. In summary, the key aspects of differentiation are that it needs to:

- be viewed within the learning and curriculum in context;

- be varied – differentiation for one group of learners might be quite different for another group;

- take into account factors such as the learning environment, the content, the process and the outcomes of learning.

## Features of learning styles

Many of the dimensions and features of learning styles models are quite similar, showing only subtle differences. As indicated earlier, the approaches often focus on left- and right-hemisphere processing styles, that is the analytical and the holistic features of information processing. For example, in the cognitive model developed by Riding and Cheema (1991) and Riding and Rayner (1998), the four dimensions are analyst, wholist, verbaliser and imager. The analyst would prefer to process information in small pieces, can work well independently and likes to learn in a linear logical manner. The wholist needs to have a view of the whole picture, works well with others and will prefer to work within a framework. The verbaliser prefers to express information in words rather than pictures and the imager works best from diagrams and pictures and has good social skills but may need some support with structure. Riding and Rayner, through the use of the Cognitive Styles Analysis (Riding, 1991), show how these dimensions combine, making four combinations possible – analytic-verbaliser, analytic-imager, wholist-verbaliser and wholist-imager.

These dimensions, although cognitive dimensions, have similarities with many other models and approaches in cognitive and learning styles. For example, in the Kolb approach (Kolb, 1976) there are two learning dimensions. These are concrete experience/reflective observation –

the former relates to learning from specific experiences and relating to people; reflective observation, on the other hand, involves making judgements and having different perspectives by looking for the meaning of things. The other dimension is abstract conceptualization/active experimentation. The former focuses on logical analysis of ideas and the intellectual understanding of a situation, while active experimentation relates to the ability to get things done, risk-taking and action-type activities. Using Kolb's model the two dimensions can relate to four learning types. The Type I learner is primarily a 'hands-on' learner, tends to rely on intuition rather than logic and enjoys applying learning in real-life situations.

The Type II learner likes to look at things from many points of view, would rather watch than take action, likes to use imagination in problem-solving and is sensitive to feelings when learning. The Type III learner likes solving problems and finding practical solutions and uses for learning but is not too comfortable in social and interpersonal issues and prefers technical tasks. The Type IV learner is concise and logical, prefers abstract ideas and concepts than people issues; practicality is less important than a sound logical explanation.

The easiest strategies to implement in the classroom are the visual, auditory, kinaesthetic/tactile approaches. These can be built into what can simply be termed 'good teaching'.

## Visual/auditory/tactile – some guidelines

Auditory learners would benefit from:

- sounding out words in reading;
- verbal instructions;
- the use of tapes;
- rehearsing information, repeating it many times to get the sound.

Visual learners would benefit from:

- the use of visual diagrams;
- use of video, flashcards, charts and maps;
- practising visualising words and ideas;
- writing out notes for frequent and quick visual scan and review.

Kinaesthetic/tactile learners would benefit from:

- tracing words as they are being spoken;
- learning facts by writing them out several times;
- moving around while studying;
- taking risks in learning;
- making written notes but also discussing these with others;
- making study plans.

# Why the inclusive context?

This question relates to the title of this book. Why should learning styles be set against the inclusive context? Simply, it does not have to be! Learning styles can be very effective in a special school or educational provision that is not viewed as inclusive. Inclusive education, however, has the potential to promote approaches that can be seen as enlightening and progressive with a focus on learning as well as teaching. This is highlighted below.

## Traditional approach

- Focus on student

- Assessment of student by specialist

- Diagnostic process

- Prescriptive tasks

- Set student programme

- Selection and streaming

- Placement on programmes depend on assessed abilities

## Inclusive approach

- Focus on classroom

- Reflection on teaching process

- Examining learning factors

- Collaborative problem-solving

- Development of strategies

- Adaptive classroom environment

  (adapted from Porter, 1997)

The factors under the heading 'inclusive approach' are considerably more consistent than those under the 'traditional approach' heading. Learning styles can therefore be seen as part of the strategies and processes used to ensure that inclusion is effective in mainstream and regular classes. The diversity of learners found in an inclusive setting almost lends itself to ensuring that learning styles be part of the process of accommodating to all learners.

Brechin (2004) issues some caution on 'differentiation by task', indicating that it can be demotivating for some students, especially those who have a learning difficulty such as dyslexia. Such students may be faced with tasks that are certainly achievable but these may not necessarily reflect their abilities, and they will feel under-fulfilled. As an alternative Brechin reports on McNamara and Moreton's (1997) model of differentiation. This model is based not on a hierarchy of abilities but on collaboration between children with different learning styles and learning strengths. McNamara and Moreton argue that such collaboration leads to effective thinking and this in turn motivates all learners and can increase the amount of spontaneous learning taking place. In this model students are encouraged to record information in a variety of ways and not solely in written form. This is similar to the multiple intelligence approaches described earlier in this book. One of the key differences is that in the McNamara and Moreton approach, the students themselves are the collaborators and they, perhaps with prompting, develop their preferred approach. This is both dynamic and metacognitive because it puts the onus onto the student and encourages reflection and experimentation. Risk-taking in the learning situation is something that many students are reluctant to get too involved in. Many students, partly because of the traditional aspects of the education system and the need to pass exams as a way of demonstrating achievement and success, often opt for the cautious and safe approach. In some cases that could be the pure memorising of facts. In an interview study of senior pupils in an attempt to find out their awareness of learning styles, almost all the respondents mentioned passing exams. In other words, they equated learning styles, not with learning efficiency, but as a means of passing exams (Lucas, personal correspondence, 2005).

It is crucial that if schools are to develop learning-friendly environments based on learning styles, equity and creativity, they have to move from what Senge (2000) refers to as the 'industrial-age assumptions' about learning and schools. These include: children are deficient and schools fix them; learning takes place in the head and not in the body as a whole; everyone learns or should learn in the same way; learning takes place in the classroom, not in the world; there are smart kids and there are dumb kids; and competition accelerates learning. Although many of these assumptions seem absurd, many practices in schools are based on these and this is one of the principal barriers to implementing learning styles in a widespread way throughout the education system. MacGilchrist et al. (2004) argue strongly against these industrial-age assumptions. They suggest that 'an emphasis on performance without attending to learning will not achieve the goals we need for education in the twenty-first century … what we need are learning–centred classrooms which are not to be confused with child-centred classrooms' (p142). This emphasises that implementing learning styles on its own is not sufficient and it certainly is not the responsibility of one teacher. The success of learning-centred classrooms and the use of learning styles are dependent on many of the systemic features of a school. MacGilchrist et al. report on the concept of corporate intelligence and relate that to 'intelligent schools'. They argue that an intelligent school has the capacity to mobilise all within the school and can transform vision into action. They identify the concepts, principles and attributes of nine factors that they call the 'nine intelligences' (p111). One of these intelligences is systemic intelligence. It is this intelligence that relates to how a school works, the thinking behind the system and the manner of organisation. These are crucial considerations for the successful implementation of learning styles. MacGilchrist et al. argue that it is this systemic intelligence that is responsible for ensuring that vision and action work together.

## Concluding comment

It is clear there is no one formula or solution for tackling the issue of implementing learning styles in classrooms. There are many barriers, some of which have been identified here, such as the diversity found among students and the time and classroom management conflicts that are features of teaching in today's classrooms. It is important therefore to operate from one's standpoint of comfort, to locate a model or models that can be accommodated within the class and, most importantly, are meaningful to students. It is also important to enter into dialogue with students about their learning and their learning style. It is this information that can be the most useful in the development of learning tasks and materials for all.

## Chapter 8 Overview

# Learning Styles in the Inclusion Context

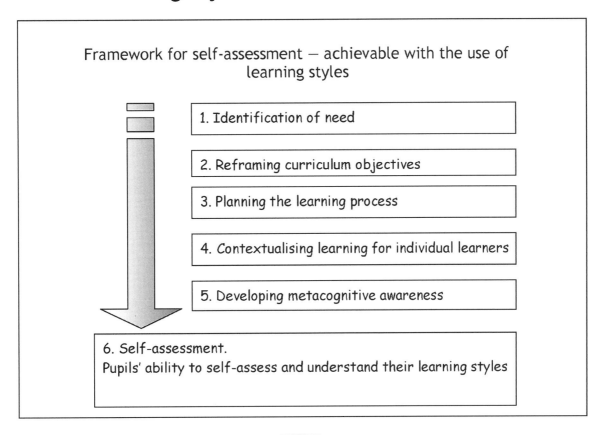

Framework for self-assessment — achievable with the use of learning styles

1. Identification of need

2. Reframing curriculum objectives

3. Planning the learning process

4. Contextualising learning for individual learners

5. Developing metacognitive awareness

6. Self-assessment.
Pupils' ability to self-assess and understand their learning styles

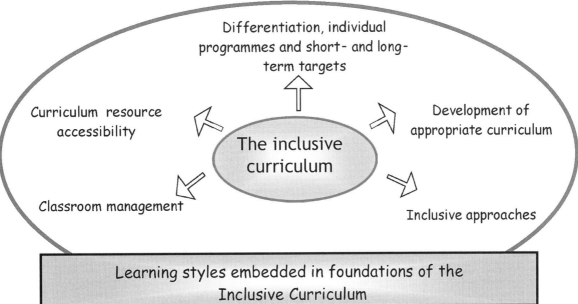

Differentiation, individual programmes and short- and long-term targets

Curriculum resource accessibility

Development of appropriate curriculum

The inclusive curriculum

Classroom management

Inclusive approaches

Learning styles embedded in foundations of the Inclusive Curriculum

PART 4

# EFFECTIVE LEARNING

# Promoting Effective Learning

**Outline of chapter and key points**

This chapter

- looks at promoting effective learning through curriculum development;
- provides examples of a range of motivating strategies;
- highlights how learning styles should be considered within the processes of planning and implementing effective learning.

Key points

- Mind mapping can be used to brainstorm as well as to organise and remember information.
- Effective learning requires resourcefulness rather then resources.
- Student ownership over learning can promote effective learning and develop metacognitive strategies.
- Students need to be encouraged to reflect on the activities they have been involved in and to evaluate how effective the activity was for them.
- Learning skills need to be linked with curriculum content and curriculum objectives.
- Talk and active learning can fuel independent thinking, creativity and independence in learning.
- Thinking-centred instruction should aim to help students become self-regulated learners.
- All learning competencies should be achievable.
- Learning styles can act as a catalyst to promote more enlightened approaches to teaching and learning.
- In order for learners to gain insights into their learning, constant feedback is crucial.

Learning styles can be a catalyst for promoting effective learning. It is likely, and not altogether surprising, that through the use of learning styles students will learn more effectively and efficiently. That view, however, is not universally accepted (Coffield, 2005). Nevertheless, whatever the arguments, learning styles can very likely engage the learner in a reflective range of strategies and approaches to learning. The use of learning styles can provoke the learner, and the teacher, to reflect on aspects of learning and to consider different learning strategies.

This chapter will discuss a range of these alternative strategies and evaluate their appropriateness within an inclusive context.

# Mind Mapping®

The ideas behind Mind Maps® were developed by Tony Buzan (www.buzan.org). Mind maps can be an effective method of note taking and useful for the development and generation of ideas through associations. Mind maps can therefore be used to brainstorm as well as to organise and recall information. There is now a plethora of books on mind maps aimed at all sectors of learning both in education and industry.

According to Buzan, the key features of mind maps are:

- organisation;

- key words;

- association;

- clustering;

- visual memory – print the key words, use colour, symbols, icons, 3D effects, arrows and outlining groups of words;

- outstandingness – every mind map needs a unique centre;

- conscious involvement.

Mind maps therefore can help learners organise information and the direct link between different pieces of information can be noted. This link helps with recall of information. At a glance one should be able to pick out the key words in a mind map. Additionally, the learner who is compiling the mind map has to train him/herself to think of the key words and ideas. Mind maps therefore can be a study aid to help the learner identify the key areas that are of the most importance.

One of the other concepts underlying mind maps is that of association. Associations can trigger ideas and links with other information to be learned. This in fact is one of the central purposes and why mind maps can be useful for brainstorming.

## Developing a mind map

Buzan (2003) suggests that to make a mind map, it is preferable to start in the centre of the page with the main idea, and then work outwards in all directions, producing a growing and organised structure composed of key words and key images. Mind maps are not developed in a linear way but rather are based on ideas and associations. Figure 9.1 is a mind map of how you may use this book.

You will note that in Figure 9.1 the central image is the book, *Learning Styles and Inclusion*. From that central image the key ideas for how it can be used are staff development, classroom practice, staff discussion, curriculum development, assessment strategies, developing school ethos, and the school environment. From each of these points other ideas can be developed. For example, staff discussion can lead to a formal school working group on learning styles, looking at how they can become integrated into the different curriculum policies of the school. This could lead on to assessment re-evaluation and the introduction of new resources. This may lead to discussion and involvement with parents.

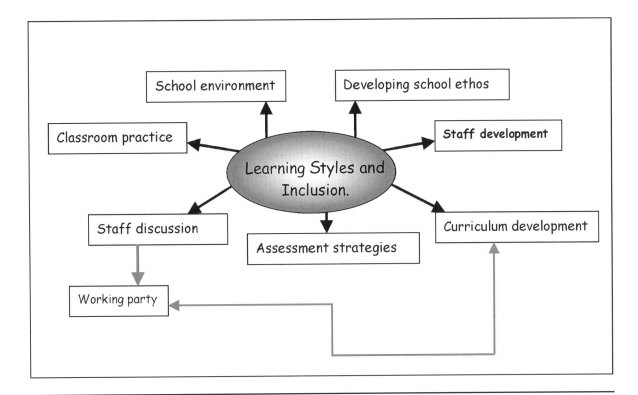

**Figure 9.1 A framework for Learning Styles and Inclusion**

So every word or idea used in the mind map can be linked to other ideas, and these can link to other ideas and concepts. This can provide an element of creativity and originality and can assist with lateral thinking. This is why mind maps can be useful for brainstorming. Although the mind maps used in this book are in black and white, most people use colour when developing a mind map as this can provide a clearer overview and highlight the range of connections related to the subject.

Buzan (2003) suggests that our brains tend to look for patterns and completion. This, according to Buzan, leads to 'radiant thinking', which refers to 'associative thought processes that proceed from, or connect to, a central point … and although the mind map is drawn on a two dimensional page it represents a multidimensional reality, encompassing space, time and colour' (p57).

Kline (1988), in his book the *Everyday Genius*, voices support for the use of mind maps. He suggests that mind mapping combined with visual thinking can effectively raise intelligence. Visual thinking can enhance creativity and allow an individual to identify the material that has to be learned and understood. This can also promote control over learning as well as lateral and creative thinking.

## Classroom activities

Effective learning requires resourcefulness rather then resources. Resources are constrained by budgetary requirements but resourcefulness is wide open and the teacher, given the time, space and opportunity, can promote and provide a stimulating and resourceful learning environment for all children. There are many examples of this in the literature. The field of accelerated learning, in particular, has for some time been an expanding one (see the Accelerated Learning website www.accelerated-learning.co.uk for examples of resources on brain-based teaching, thinking skills, multiple intelligence, school leadership, behaviour management, emotional intelligence, mind mapping, maths, music and movement, special needs, talented and gifted children, parenting as well as a range of interactive software on the theme of learning strategies).

## Games

One of the most effective ranges of strategies are those developed by Paul Ginnis in *The Teacher's Toolkit* (Ginnis, 2002). Ginnis uses many guiding principles in his work and refers to a range of learning theories and different models of learning styles. One of the key points highlighted by Ginnis is that 'learners are more motivated, engaged and open when they have some control over their learning' (p30). He suggests a five-point formula for achieving this, which includes the need to provide novelty and variety to sustain attention; the importance of ensuring that the learner's basic needs are met such as food, drink and a comfortable environment for learning; the need to ensure that students have an understanding of the big picture, that is ensuring they know the purpose of the lesson and how it fits in with what has gone on before; and the need to plan with learners. It is this planning, according to Ginnis, that is the route to ownership. This point has been indicated a number of times throughout this book: ownership over learning can promote more effective learning and develop metacognitive strategies. These strategies can make learning more meaningful and enhance the transfer of learning, thus making the learning process more efficient. Ginnis provides a recipe for effective learning which involves:

- thinking skills;

- emotional intelligence;

- independence, interdependence;

- multi-sensation – that is, ensuring all the senses are being used;

- fun – students need to enjoy learning and articulation of ideas;

- opportunities to engage in discussion and brainstorming of ideas.

Ginnis suggests that these factors should be integral to the design of classroom activities.

One of Ginnis's many activities in *The Teacher's Toolkit* is 'one to one', a peer teaching activity that involves pairing students in a learning activity that involves one teaching the topic to the other. This simple activity incorporates metacognitive principles such as self-monitoring and self-direction and can be used to include differentiated extension work. Another similar activity is the 'discussion carousel' in which learners sit in chairs in two concentric circles, an outer and an inner of equal numbers. Facing pairs are given a topic to discuss and a time deadline and then have to summarise their partner's contribution to neighbouring pairs and then the process begins again in rotation with fresh topics. Many have experienced this as a popular ice-breaker activity, but as a structured classroom activity there are many useful teaching and learning points to be obtained. These include listening skills, summarising skills, peer interaction, turn-taking, reflection and ownership over learning.

There is no doubt the types of activities suggested by Ginnis are certainly fun and motivating. Furthermore, they incorporate essential learning principles and usually involve and incorporate a range of learning styles. Nevertheless, it is important that all students are encouraged to reflect on the game activity and to evaluate how effective the game was for them and how their learning developed as a result. This part is as important – perhaps more important – than the actual activity itself. Some examples follow.

| Learner's self-questions | Learning and teaching points |
|---|---|
| What did I do during the activity? | Recall of information, sequencing of activities |
| What did my partner or others in the class do? | Observation of others, awareness of the role of others in class activity |
| How did I tackle the task? | Awareness of learning process |
| What help did I need? | Awareness of resources, contributions from others, group needs |
| What help did I give others? | Social skills, interaction, motivating others |
| How effective was I as a learner? | Metacognitive skills, self-monitoring and self-assessment |
| How do I know this? | Task awareness, awareness of purpose of task |
| What skills have I developed as a result of this activity? | Self-awareness, task awareness, enhanced awareness of the learning process |
| How can I use these skills in future learning? | Learning transfer, other subjects and topics. |

## Learning Toolkit

The above points are highlighted in the excellent two-volume *Learning Toolkit* developed by Fil Came et al. (2002a, b) published by Learning Works (www.learning-works.org.uk). The *Toolkit* encapsulates many of the learning principles and models indicated above. Volume 1 has units on personal learning, learning styles, multiple intelligences, emotional literacy and communication skills. Volume 2 looks at study skills, memory trainers, energisers, thinking skills and team skills.

The *Toolkit* highlights the need to link learning skills with curriculum content and curriculum objectives. For example, the unit on study skills in Volume 2 has activities relating to the importance of water. This is part of a unit on healthy food and from that a number of linked activities are prepared and the learning objectives stemming from these are indicated. These include instruction, information, persuasion, explanation, recount, evaluation and analysis. The connections are made with healthy food to water and to Egyptian society and seasons. The activity on this topic begins with what the authors call 'topic sentences'. These are the key ideas and facts from each paragraph. Another activity turns these topic sentences into bullet points and the bullet points are turned into a memory map. This activity also provides the learner with a sense of control and purpose over the learning experience. Importantly, however, it is set within curriculum content and the outcome of the activity will promote knowledge as well as the other learning skills the authors mention throughout the *Toolkit*, such as analysis and evaluation.

In Volume 1 on personal learning the link is between the learning skills and the learning models that underpin these skills, all set in a practical format. For example, in 'communication skills' the work of Rivers and the seven-challenges approach is drawn upon. The authors have adapted these to five areas, each of which fosters communication skills. These are in five steps – co-operate, actively listen, explain yourself clearly, appreciate more often and request information and needs specifically. Each of these has user-friendly and clearly presented activities on the full range of the learning skills to be developed. Figure 9.2 shows one example of this from the section on 'explain yourself clearly'.

**Name:**

# *Explain*: 16 Conversation Hints

### A. Opinion Statements

1. 'I think that…'
2. My opinion is…'
3. I disagree with what you've said because…
4. I agree with your first point, but…

### B. Breaking into an Ongoing Conversation

1. Listen actively – nod, look directly at others, say 'uh-huh'.
2. Wait for a natural pause in the conversation.
3. Raise your voice slightly to signal others you wish to speak.
4. Use your body – lean forward into the conversational arena; use hand gestures; touch the person on the arm.
5. State an opinion: 'I think that…', or ask a question: 'What about'.
6. Use the person's name to gain attention: 'Tom, I also think…'.

### C. Resisting Interruption

1. Raise your voice slightly to signal that you would like to finish your comment.
2. Repeat your opening phrase so that you don't lose your train of thought: 'I think… but I do think that…'.
3. Continue talking without hesitation.
4. Don't look at the interrupter; look at those who are attentive.
5. Ask the interrupter to wait until you have finished your statement: 'Please wait a minute'.
6. Hold up your hand or touch the person to signal that you would like the interrupter to stop.

**Figure 9.2 Conversation hints**

## Multicultural factors

It is important to ensure that learning experiences in learning toolkits are multicultural. Knowing and understanding other cultures is an important learning prerequisite for appreciating other points of view and understanding the non-verbal and language customs of different countries. In the *Toolkit* there are activities that focus on this, such as the one below.

| Custom in country | UK | USA | Pakistan | Mexico |
|---|---|---|---|---|
| Greetings<br>Touching<br>Eye contact<br>Older people<br>Eating routines | | | | |

(from Came et al., 2002)

## Opening minds

One of the purposes of the learning experience is to open children's minds. Quite often the learning experience can be a restrictive one and rather than open minds can actually close them, and much of the excitement and pleasure of learning can be lost. This point has been highlighted by Jane Healy in a number of her books but particularly in the book *How to Have Intelligent and Creative Conversations with Your Kids* (Healy, 1992). Healy emphasises the importance of talk and active learning. Talk and active learning can fuel independent thinking, creativity and independence in learning. Healy provides the interesting example of a demotivated child; the cause of the demotivation was generally thought to be due to a specific learning difficulty – implying that the child had a difficulty in learning. Healy in fact found that the child's main difficulty was that he had not had the opportunity to think. His life and learning at home and school did not promote thinking opportunities – students were not encouraged to disagree, discuss issues or even to ask questions. Before a child's mind can be opened to learning, he/she must be inspired and motivated to learn. This can be achieved by recognising and seizing learning opportunities that promote thinking and enhance independent learning. Healy uses the quote to support her hypothesis – 'we learn more by looking for the answer to a question and not finding it than we do from learning the answer itself' (Healy, 1992, p33). The basis of this is to develop children's self-confidence by encouraging them to question and to help them realise that there may not be one right answer to a problem.

Healy also provides ideas to develop talk. She believes that talk is the basis of intelligent thinking and the development of creativity and skills in learning. Some of the talk tactics described by Healy are shown below.

- Acknowledging
  - That's a new idea
  - I see
  - Interesting point

- Restating
  - You want to know ...?
  - Does that mean ...?
  - Are you saying ...?
  - So you are disagreeing with ...?
  - You think ...?

- Clarifying
  - Why do you say that?
  - I don't quite understand what you mean.
  - What are we really discussing here?
  - That seems to relate to ...

- Disagreeing
  - You make an interesting point, have you considered ...?
  - Is it possible that ...?
  - Here's another thought ...

- Challenging thinking
  - I wonder how we know ...?
  - Can you give some reasons for ...?

- Redirecting
  - How does that relate to ...?
  - Good point but have we finished discussing ...?

- Expanding
  - I wonder what else this could relate to ...?

(adapted from Healy, 1992)

The key underlying message in the above is the need to open learners' minds and to extend and expand their thinking. Talk and enquiry-based learning are both means of achieving this and both can be accommodated within a learning styles approach. The key point is that schools that are open to learning styles are usually also aware of the importance of talk and enquiry. Both form part of the learning ethos and this ethos is necessary for effective learning.

# Thinking-centred instruction

## Instrumental Enrichment

The model developed by Feuerstein and his associates – Instrumental Enrichment – (Feuerstein et al., 1980) focuses on an approach that can be described as structural cognitive modifiability. Feuerstein first drew the distinction between manifest performance and underlying potential in his seminal work, *The Dynamic Assessment of Retarded Performers* (1979), in which he introduced the notion of 'dynamic', as opposed to 'static', assessment by means of the Learning Potential Assessment Device. He argues for a total rethink of the way in which assessment is carried out, based on focusing on the interaction between the child and the teacher.

The Instrumental Enrichment Programme consists of 14 sets of cognitive activities, each of which is aimed at the development of one or another aspect of efficient and effective cognitive functioning. It can be used as part of the inclusive school curriculum, or as the basis for an individualised intervention process.

Feuerstein's theory suggests that cognitive deficiencies are not considered to be permanent traits but aspects of current inefficient performance that can be improved by means of mediated learning experiences (Kozulin and Rand, 2000).

## Self-regulated learning

Andrade (1999) discusses thinking-centred instruction that aims to help students become self-regulated learners. These consist of four instructional approaches and represent some of the research and products of the Harvard Cognitive Skills Group. These are:

- Thinking Through Thinkpoints – this aims to help teachers and students identify topics or ideas within the curriculum and encourages students to explore those topics in critical and creative ways.

- Thinking Through Dispositions – this aims to enrich and deepen understanding by cultivating not only students' thinking skills, but also their inclinations, attitudes, and habits of mind.

- Thinking Through Transfer – this aims to secure and deepen learning by activating and connecting students' knowledge to topics and subject areas both in and out of school.

- Thinking Through Assessment – this aims to improve thinking performances and deepen understanding through the design and employment of thinking-centred assessment.

The important point is that this approach takes thinking skills into the complete learning environment – from curriculum development to assessment. It can generate thinking and problem-solving skills, develop good study habits based on thinking and facilitate transfer of skills to other subject areas of the curriculum. It has already been noted that many students actually do not know how to think as they have not had sufficient practice in this skill. Additionally it is often the case that thinking skills are seen as an add-on to the curriculum but not the central focus as is the case with this approach.

# Developing learning competencies

Two factors are of importance here – one is the word 'developing' and the other 'learning competencies'. Taking the phrase 'learning competencies', the question we need to ask ourselves is 'competent in relation to what'? For example, there are many young people who are competent in kicking a ball and have learned this skill over time but they are not competent compared with the professional soccer player. Competencies need therefore to be matched to the learner and their Zone of Proximal Development (see Chapter 1). This means that all competencies should be achievable. The difference, however, between 'learning' and 'competencies' needs to be made clear. One can achieve the competencies without necessarily having gone through the learning process. In the phrase 'learning competencies' the key word is 'learning' as it is important that learning actually takes place and that the learner is aware of how that learning was acquired.

There is no question, however, that learning does not automatically appear but is a developmental process. The word 'developing' implies a type of nurturing processing that takes time. It needs to be understood that learning also takes time and during that time the learner undertakes a number of learning processes relating to his/her understanding of the material. The well known Bloom's (1956) taxonomy – knowledge, analysis, synthesis, hypothesis and evaluation – is an example of that development, but each of these stages in itself has also developmental phases. The work of Piaget and Vygotsky, on constructivism and social constructivism, highlight the important role that 'developmental stages' play in the acquisition of learning competencies. Nevertheless, it is important that developmental stages should not impose an unnecessary restriction on the development of learning competencies. There is a strong indication from the literature on learning styles, multiple intelligences and thinking skills that children are very likely much more capable than we give them credit for.

Bransford et al. (2000) suggest that the word 'development' needs to be more firmly understood in educational terms. They maintain that this term is critical to understanding the changes in children's conceptual growth. This implies that cognitive development does not result from the gathering of knowledge but from the processes involved in cognitive reorganisation. One of the underlying points from *How People Learn* (Bransford et al., 2000) is that we do not give young children enough credit for their ability to develop metacognitive skills. The authors suggest that children can develop metacognitive skills very early on and are able to plan and monitor their success and correct errors when necessary. But these abilities for learning need to be nurtured and are dependent on catalysts and mediation. Teachers and all adults play a critical role, according to Bransford et al., in 'promoting children's curiosity, by directing children's attention, structuring their experiences, supporting their learning attempts and regulating the complexity and difficulty of levels of information' (pp234–5).

One of the themes of this book is that learning styles can act as a catalyst and promote more enlightened approaches to teaching and learning. The development of learning competencies does not end with the assessment grade or the end of the topic – that is only the beginning. As Bransford et al. point out, a major goal of schooling is to prepare for flexible adaptation to new problems and new settings. Learning competencies can only have been achieved when the learner is able to transfer what they have learned to new situations. This transfer can include the transfer of concepts, the transfer of information from one school subject to another, from one school year to another and from school to non-school activities. Bransford et al. suggest that people's ability to transfer depends on the threshold of initial learning they have acquired as this must be sufficient to support transfer. They also emphasise that spending a lot of time on a task is not in itself sufficient. Much depends on how learners use that time. Learners need to monitor their learning and actively consider how they are progressing with the task, and the strategies they are using. Interestingly, they suggest that children are more likely to be able to learn more effectively and be able to transfer information more successfully if they are taught in a multi-context situation. Therefore information taught in a conventional subject-by-subject manner will not be as effective for transfer as materials taught in a thematic fashion where the students are encouraged to grasp the underlying principles and concepts.

The key point therefore for the student in relation to developing learning competencies is the question 'how do I know this?' This is the question the learner needs to ask him/herself throughout the learning experience. Additionally, in order for learners to gain insights into their learning, constant feedback is crucial. This could be feedback from others and feedback from themselves. This metacognitive process helps learners not only to develop transferable competencies, but also to find out about themselves as learners. It is this self-knowledge that will provide the most useful and effective tool in future learning as they will be able to monitor, regulate and adapt their own understanding of new learning in different learning contexts.

This process involves more than students learning but should revolve round the complete learning environment and the learning and teaching experience. Brown and Campione (1994) highlight this when discussing the key principles of effective teaching and learning. They suggest that students should be encouraged to be self-reflective. The environment, they argue, should be designed to foster intentional learning, not programmes, to encourage student reflection and discussion and the mode of discussion should focus on the students' ability to discover and use knowledge.

## The role of schema

'Schema' refers to the development of a conceptual framework that can help the learner organise information into a meaningful context. This can aid understanding and recall. The development of a schema also helps the learner organise and categorise information. It helps the learner utilise the background and the existing knowledge he/she has on a subject. This in itself can aid comprehension and recall as the new knowledge is being assimilated into the student's current schema or reframed and accommodated into a new schema.

When children read a story or a passage, they need to relate this to their existing framework of knowledge – i.e. their own schema. So when coming across new knowledge, learners try to fit it into their existing framework of knowledge based on previous learning, which is the schema they possess for that topic or piece of information. It is important for the teacher to find out how developed a child's schema is on a particular topic, before providing more and new information. Being aware of this will help the teacher ensure the child develops appropriate understanding of the new information. The key points about the passage could help the reader understand the information more readily and provide a framework into which the reader can slot ideas and meaning from the passage. The development of a schema can help the learner:

- attend to the incoming information;
- provide a scaffolding for memory;

- make inferences from the passage which also aid comprehension and recall;

- utilise his/her previous knowledge.

There are a number of strategies which can help in the development of a schema. An example of this can be seen in an examination of a framework for a story. In such a framework two principal aspects can be identified: the structure of the story and the details related to the components of the structure.

The structure of a story can be seen in the following components:

- background;

- context;

- characters;

- beginning;

- main part;

- events;

- conclusion.

The details that may relate to these components can be recalled by asking appropriate questions. Taking the background as an example, one can see how appropriate questioning can help the learner build up a schema to facilitate understanding of the rest of the story:

- What was the weather like?

- Where did the story take place?

- Describe the scene.

- What were the main colours?

## Background knowledge

Background knowledge is an important aid to comprehension. Although background knowledge in itself is insufficient to facilitate new learning, it can be interwoven with the new material that is being learnt. It is important that the learner is able to use the new information in different and unfamiliar situations. Hence the connections between the reader's background knowledge and the new information must be highlighted in order for the learner to incorporate the new knowledge in a meaningful manner.

The ideas contained in a text therefore must be linked in some way to the reader's background knowledge and the ideas need to be presented in a coherent and sequential manner. Such coherence and sequencing of ideas at the learning stage not only allows the material to be retained and recalled, but also facilitates effective comprehension. Being aware of the learner's prior knowledge of a lesson is of fundamental importance. Before embarking on new material prior knowledge can be linked with the new ideas, in order to pave the way for effective study techniques and strategies to enhance comprehension and recall.

# Reciprocal teaching and scaffolding

Reciprocal teaching refers to a procedure which both monitors and enhances comprehension by focusing on processes relating to questioning, clarifying, summarising and predicting (Palincsar and Brown, 1984). This is an interactive process and one that is initially led by the teacher. The teacher leads the discussion by asking questions and this generates additional questions from participants; the questions are then clarified by teacher and participants together. The discussion is then summarised by teacher or participants, then a new 'teacher' is selected by the participants to lead the discussion on the next section of the text.

## Scaffolding

The procedure described above can be referred to as 'scaffolding', in which a scaffold or supports are built to develop the understanding of text. This may be in the form of the teacher either providing the information or generating appropriate responses through questioning and clarifying. The supports are then withdrawn gradually, when the learner has achieved the necessary understanding to continue with less support.

Cudd and Roberts (1994) observed that poor readers were not automatically making the transfer from book language to their own writing. As a result the students' writing lacked the precise vocabulary and varied syntax that was evident during reading. To overcome this difficulty Cudd and Roberts introduced a scaffolding technique to develop both sentence sense and vocabulary. They focused on sentence expansion by using vocabulary from the children's readers and using these as sentence stems that encouraged sentence expansion. Thus the procedure involved:

- selection of vocabulary from basal reader;

- embedding this vocabulary into sentence stems;

- selecting particular syntactic structures to introduce the stem;

- embedding the targeted vocabulary into sentence stems to produce complex sentences;

- discussing the sentence stems, including the concepts involved;

- completing a sentence using the stems;

- repeating the completed sentence providing oral reinforcement of both the vocabulary and the sentence structure;

- encouraging the illustration of some of their sentences, helping to give the sentence a specific meaning.

Cudd and Roberts have found that this sentence expansion technique provides a scaffold for children to help develop their sentence structure and vocabulary. Examination of writing samples of the students revealed development in vocabulary choice and sentence variety. The children, including those with reading and writing difficulties, were seen to gain better control over the writing process and gained confidence from using their own ideas and personal experiences.

# Retelling as an instructional and assessment tool

Ulmer and Timothy (2001) developed an alternative assessment framework based on retelling as an instructional and assessment tool. This indicated that informative assessment of a child's comprehension could take place by using criteria relating to how the child retells a story. Ulmer and Timothy suggested the following criteria:

- textual – what the child remembered;

- cognitive – how the child processed the information;

- affective – how the child felt about the text.

Their two-year study indicated that 100 per cent of the teachers in the study assessed for textual information, only 31 per cent looked for cognitive indicators and 25 per cent for affective. Yet the teachers who did go beyond the textual found rich information. Some examples of information provided by the teachers indicated that assessing beyond the textual level in relation to the use of the retelling method of assessment could provide evidence of the child's 'creative side' and they discovered that children could go 'beyond the expectations when given the opportunity'. This is a good example of how looking for alternative means of assessing can link with the child's understandings of text and promote development thinking. It can be suggested that assessment instruments are often based on restrictive criteria, examining what the child may be expected to know, often at a textual level, but may ignore other rich sources of information which can inform about the child's thinking, both cognitive and affective, and provide suggestions for teaching.

This highlights the need to embed strategies into a context and that the context used here is the assessment of the learning competencies of the student. Assessment should always be linked in some way to instruction and one of the difficulties with some study skills programmes and strategies is that they are not linked – they stand often in isolation. The development of learning competencies, which is the key theme of this section, should not be isolated from the assessment, nor the instruction and the skills that are to be utilised and developed.

This is particularly important for students with any type of difficulty. For example, Mortimore (2003) shows how learning style can be combined with learning strategies and used effectively for children with dyslexia, even though it is accepted that not all students with dyslexia will have the same learning style nor be able to access the same types of learning strategies. Mortimore provides strategies for wholistic and for analytic learners who have dyslexia. The key point is that the assessment should inform the strategy that is to be used and it should also inform the nature of the learning process. This chapter is about effective learning, but in order for this to become a reality effective assessment and the identification of needs have to take place.

## Chapter 9 Overview
# Promoting Effective Learning

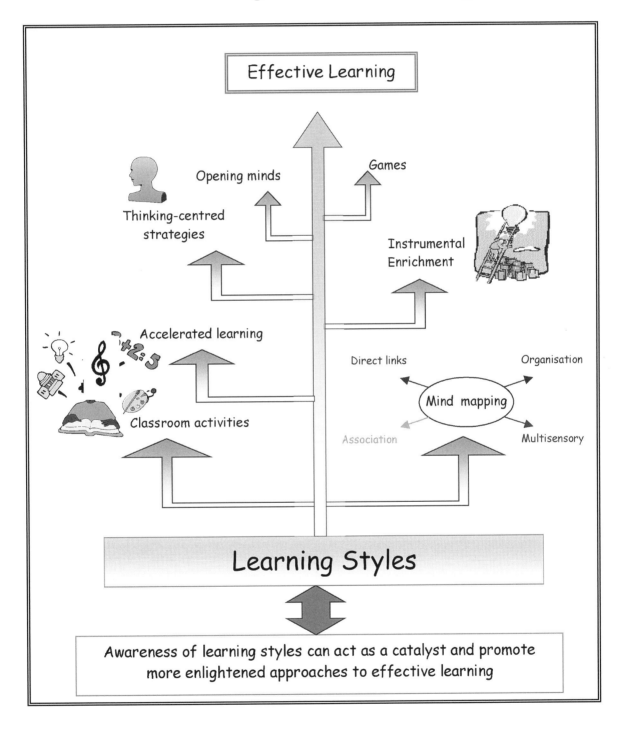

# CHAPTER 10

# Learning Styles – Strategies and Insights

> **Outline of chapter and key points**
>
> This chapter
>
> - provides an overview of learning strategies and relates these to learning styles;
> - discusses some personal insights learners have on their own learning style and strategies;
> - identifies the barriers to implementing learning styles in schools and how these can be overcome.
>
> Key points
>
> - All children are capable of learning and it is too easy to underestimate the potential of learners.
> - Many strategies for learning can be described as brain based and aim to help the learner make full use of their learning potential, but a great deal of learning is determined by the environment.
> - To be fully effective, learning strategies should be embedded in the classroom and curriculum activities.
> - Study skills programmes can, and should, be implemented as early as possible.
> - Learners need to take responsibility for their own learning.
> - The type of study aids students use will depend very much on their learning style.
> - A strategy is essentially a method of ensuring learners' strengths are being used.
> - Learning does not just happen; the learner has to make it happen.

## The brain bases of learning

The capacity of the brain to store information is unlimited. Yet the most significant factor in learning is often failure to recall. It is necessary to have a degree of recall in order to process new information and to use the strategies and principles acquired in previous learning. One of the dynamic and growth areas in the learning literature is in the field of accelerated learning – that is, using the brain more efficiently to learn more effectively. There is a growing body of research on the brain and with magnetic imaging techniques it is now easier to understand and to explain how the brain works. Taking the brain research into account, perhaps three points are of particular relevance for this book. These are:

1. All brains are **capable of learning** and this must raise questions about the concept of learning difficulties.

2. Brain cells (neurons) are **constantly changing and making new connections** with other cells and groups of cells. There will be trillions of connections at any one time but some of these connections will become redundant if they are not used and others will become stronger with learning. Edelman (1992) discusses the theory of 'neuronal group selection', which indicates that groups of neural circuits become specialised; e.g. some dealing with emotions, some with social situations and others with sensory processing. If young children are deprived of practice in social situations then they will become less competent in these situations because they will not have the neural connections to support learning and behaviour in this context.

3. Although it is well known that there is a genetic code and genetic mechanisms that can determine the nature of the neural formations in the brain, the impact and the use this is put to is **largely determined by the environment**. In this sense the environment is the context and the interaction that can influence the learner. The environment is much more than the physical surroundings; it includes the qualitative characteristics and the impact of those surroundings on the individual. This can be the social environment, the family, the school, the teacher and other students (see table below).

Environmental determinants for learning

| Social environment | Family | School | Teacher | Other students |
|---|---|---|---|---|
| Resources such as libraries, literacy materials, basic needs | Conversation, emotional needs, social skills, decision-making | Appropriate learning experiences, success, resources | Classroom layout, appropriate curriculum, resources, opportunities for interaction | Interaction, social skills, sense of belonging, opportunities for problem-solving |

# Brain and learning activities

There is now a large amount of games, strategies and models of learning based around 'changing the brain'. Some of these involve computer software such as 'memory booster' (www.lucid-research.com ) – this approach is aimed to help children improve their memory skills. It is a good example of a computer program that teaches flexible memory strategies and takes the child through a series of exercises that develop and extend learning skills. Additionally, companies such as Quantum Learning (www.learningforum.com) present a comprehensive model of learning that integrates educational theory with classroom implementation and has a strong focus on environmental factors. The context of the Quantum Learning FADE model is Foundation, Atmosphere, Design and Environment. Its foundation is built on the principles of the 'keys of excellence'. It holds the beliefs that all people can learn, people learn differently, and learning is effective when it is joyful, engaging and challenging. The keys of excellence include integrity, commitment, failure, success, ownership, purposeful speaking, flexibility and balance.

The Quantum Learning framework for student learning is expressed in five 'tenets of learning':

- Everything speaks: everything, from surroundings and tone of voice to distribution of materials, conveys an important message about learning.

- Everything is on purpose: everything we do has an intended purpose.

- Experience before label: students make meaning and transfer new content into long-term memory by connecting to existing schemata. Learning is best facilitated when students experience the information in some aspect before they acquire labels for what is being learned.

- Acknowledge every effort: acknowledgment of each student's effort encourages learning and experimentation.

- If it's worth learning, it's worth celebrating!: celebration provides feedback on progress and increases positive emotional associations with the learning.

## The ALPS approach

The accelerated learning in practice approach (ALPS) developed by Alistair Smith (Smith, 1998; Smith and Call, 2000; Smith et al., 2003) has made a considerable impact in schools. ALPS appears to equip teachers with more than strategies as its impact can be experienced throughout the school by staff and students. As well as providing strategies the approach looks at how to meet curriculum objectives through planning and target-setting. The approach is comprehensive and includes motivating techniques such as strategies for positive behaviour, music and movement, memory techniques and ideas for developing literacy skills. Acronyms are used to reinforce learning such as 'RAP' – recognition, affirmation and praise.

I interviewed one head teacher of a primary school that has implemented the approach, to discuss the school's approaches to learning styles in general as well as the specific impact of the ALPS approach (Meal, 2005). He suggested that to implement any type of learning styles approaches a number of key factors are necessary. The school climate and the school culture need to be switched on to learning styles. It is also important to direct attention to learning styles in the early stages – nursery/kindergarten is ideal as the situation there lends itself to kinaesthetic activities. Additionally, any learning styles approach requires planning and preparation. Staff development is important to provide the staff with the knowledge and the confidence and it is important that learning styles are built into curriculum and lesson plans. During the interview the head teacher suggested that it is best to keep it simple. The school is a large primary school with 640 students. Appreciating that there are many models of learning styles, he decided on the Visual, Auditory, Kinaesthetic approach (VAK) because it could be easily incorporated into school plans. It also complemented the ALPS approaches used in the school. He suggested that using learning styles allows the students to reflect on their learning and helps them to identify their strengths and weaknesses. It also makes them appreciate that they are active partners in the learning process. He uses the 'traffic light' system. This means that if the learner displays red they have not understood; amber means they are almost there; and green means they have it. This also means they have to teach it to someone else. It is only then that they can claim to have mastered the skills or material that is being learnt.

This is a good example of integrating learning styles into the school learning culture in a non-threatening and manageable manner. This is important as the whole staff have to be fully supportive and fully involved.

## Curriculum-focused learning

It is important that strategies are embedded in the class work and recognised in curriculum planning. This has been discussed in previous chapters. It is a delicate balance between providing the individual with learning strategies and highlighting how these can be adapted and accommodated within the school curriculum. Good examples of this can be found in the materials developed by Learning Works International (www.learning-works.org.uk), who produced a two-volume learning toolkit (discussed later in this chapter) that contains activities that relate to the actual curriculum. The work of David Lazear on multiple intelligences also has a strong curriculum focus. For example, in Lazear (1999) there are examples of curricular activities that relate directly to each of the eight intelligences, such as joint storytelling in social studies for developing interpersonal intelligence; using history to promote self-understanding and intra-personal intelligence; and understanding cultures through using naturalist intelligence. In pursuing naturalist intelligence approaches the students have lessons and discussions on culture and usually engage in project work looking at aspects of culture – such as food, environment, art and craft, architecture and typical livelihoods. These activities all lend themselves to exploration and fieldwork as well as classroom study. This presents opportunities for students to use naturalist intelligence.

## Brain Gym®

Brain Gym® is a popular series of activities designed to enhance performance in all areas by assisting whole-brain integration. Brain Gym brings together work from researchers in physical movement, education, vision and kinesiology. These movements can have a profound effect, developing the brain's neural pathways through movement (Dennison and Dennison, 2000).

Brain Gym is a component of educational kinesiology, which is a combination of applied kinesiology and traditional learning theory, although some aspects of yoga and acupressure are also evident in the programme. Dennison and Hargrove (1985) produced a series of exercises from which an individual programme can be devised for the child relating to the assessment. Many of these exercises include activities which involve crossing the midline, such as writing a figure eight in the air or cross-crawling and skip-a-cross, in which hands and legs sway from side to side. The aim is to achieve some form of body balance so that information can flow freely and be processed readily.

Kinesiology is the study of muscles and their functions and particular attention is paid to the patterns of reflex activity that link effective integration between sensory and motor responses. It has been argued (Heath, 2005; Mathews, 1993) that often children develop inappropriate patterns of responses to particular situations and that these can lock the child into inappropriate habits. Brain Gym is an increasingly popular method being used in schools all over the world (Taylor, 1998, 2002). It can be a fun activity and importantly can also be a whole-class activity.

# Study skills

Study skills can consist of a mixture of strategies selected by the individual. It can often be more effective, however, to develop study skills as a discrete learning programme or even integrate study skills within curriculum activities.

## Strategies for the individual

The first way is perhaps the simplest as there is a plethora of literature on study skills providing practical strategies that can be implemented on an individual basis. Some examples of these are given below.

*Get Better Grades – Cool Study Skills* (Agnew et al., 1995) This book consists of ideas and strategies for helping students learn more effectively. For some a collection of learning tips presented in a visual manner is excellent. Some of the visuals are presented like adverts or games for        maximum impact and will appeal to many students. But the onus is on the student to be able to use the book and to recognise how the strategies in the book might be helpful for them in relation to what they are studying. In other words, they have to recognise when and how to apply these strategies. For some students this is ideal as they have control over their learning, and are able to utilise the tips and the strategies in the way they wish. Other students, however, may need more structure and more guidance in order to incorporate study strategies into their everyday learning. The guidance the authors do give is excellent and every individual will likely gain something from this type of approach. They highlight a framework which they call a 'brain frame', which is like a personal mind map that incorporates a range of general strategies that the learner could use as a framework. These include suggestions such as: don't clutter, use visuals, organise, use highlighters or bold letters, connect ideas, use symbols, identify key words and use colour.

*Memory Trainers, Techniques, Games and Systems to Teach and Improve Memory Skills* (Came and Cooke 2001) (www.learning-works.org.uk) This consists of photocopiable resources for improving students' memory skills. As the authors state, memory for many students is the key to successful learning and therefore memory training can make a real difference to their achievements. One such example of this from Came and Cooke's Memory Trainer Manual is the game they call 'Classroom Mix-Up'. In this game everyone in the classroom has to take a good look around the classroom. The students are asked to remember the location of various objects in the room. The students go out for a break and during that time you change the location of various objects in the classroom. When the students come back into the classroom they are asked to write down all the things that have changed. This can be done with the whole class or a few members of the class at a time. This exercise can improve concentration, increase motivation and of course improve memory.

## Mnemonics

Mnemonics for many students can be a key method for remembering information. There are many examples of strategies using mnemonics that can be seen in memory manuals. For many students these are effective and can help with different types of learning needs, such as spelling rules, place names, geography and history. One of the most comprehensive manuals on mnemonics is *LEARN: Playful Techniques to Accelerate Learning* (Richards, 1993). The 'LEARN' part of the title stands for 'learning efficiently and remembering mnemonics'. Although mnemonics do have a strong visual element, Richards maintains that the technique can be used by those who are left-brain dominant as well as right. In fact left-brained students will benefit from practising mnemonics as it will encourage the use of the right hemisphere and their visual skills. Richards suggests that many children are restricted because they have not had sufficient practice in using visual skills. Yet all learning to some degree involves an element of visual skills. Such skills can make reading more enriching and can help with fluency. Richards suggests that the development of visual skills can be a classroom exercise that can help the student develop self-awareness in learning. She suggests that in order to maximise the benefit of this, the teacher needs to obtain insights into the processes children use to progress through the task to arrive at the output. She advocates that children are asked questions such as: How did you remember that? Did you label it in your mind? Did you describe it to yourself? Can you manipulate the object you are visualising? Obtaining responses to these and other similar questions can be a learning exercise for the teacher and it can provide an indication of the strategies the child is using and the level of their visual abilities.

## Revision

Many students have difficulty with planning revision and some students with global learning styles may have difficulty with revision. Essentially learners need to take responsibility for their own learning. Planning a programme for revision is very much part of that. Many students equate revision with attempting to memorise huge chunks of information, often out of context. The purpose of revision should not be to memorise the facts, but rather to ensure that the key issues and questions relating to the material are understood. Revision is as much about identifying the right questions as remembering and assimilating facts. The learner should be asking questions such as:

- Why am I studying this?

- What are the key questions relating to this topic?

- Why are these the key questions?

- What other questions can be raised about this topic?

- Why is this topic in the course?

- What is its importance?

- Have I covered the key areas?

By developing a framework for questions about the topic the learner will be able to obtain a comprehensive picture of that topic. Many learners make the mistake of starting with the facts and then trying to answer questions from the basis of the facts. A top-down approach, such as that which begins with an understanding of the whole topic, will ensure the main issues in the topic are identified and understood.

Revision can be a stressful time for many learners, but because it often takes place in isolation it does provide the opportunity for the student to experiment with his/her learning style. This highlights the benefit of knowing one's learning style and using it well before revision for major exams. It is also important to appreciate that revision is an active process. Often students measure quality of revision by the length of time they spend reading books or notes. Often short bouts of study can be more effective.

## Study aids

The type of study aids students use will depend very much on their learning style. The list below shows some of the aids that are popular with many students:

- coloured writing pens;
- colour highlighting pens;
- 'Post-it'™ notes in different shapes and colours;
- paper in different colours;
- a wall chart;
- cork board for checklists;
- Blu-Tack™ for attaching *aide-mémoires* to visible objects;
- index cards for notes;
- large paper (A3 and larger for drawing diagrams);
- space to spread out books and materials.

## Study skills programmes

A well-constructed study skills programme can do much to enhance concept development, metacognitive awareness, transfer of learning and success in the classroom. Such programmes will vary with the age and stage of the learner. A study skills programme for primary children would be different from that which may help students cope with examinations at secondary level. Well-developed study skills habits at the primary stage can provide a sound foundation for tackling new material in secondary school and help equip the student for examinations. It is worth considering the purpose and context of study skills programmes as they need to have a context and be meaningful to the student and in some way relate to the curriculum. This does not always happen. There is a vast literature on study skills providing strategies which I am sure are meaningful to the author, but they may not be as meaningful to the student. It is worth reflecting on the bulletin reported by Nisbet and Shucksmith (1986) that was produced by the Bureau of Educational Research at the University of Illinois in 1924! The bulletin suggested that training in study procedure should be based upon an understanding of the individual needs of the pupils concerned, should be designed for specific purposes and should be planned with care. Along the same lines, Marland (1981) suggested that learning to learn is rarely specified as a curriculum aim. He suggested that those planning school syllabuses seem to presume that the process of learning will be assimilated while subjects are being studied. Although these comments are dated, the advice is sound and as relevant today as it was all those years ago.

## Principal factors in study skills

Some of the principal factors in a study skills programme include the following:

- reading/spelling/writing skills;

- comprehension skills;

- listening/communication skills;

- memory skills and transfer of knowledge and skills.

### Reading skills

Reading involves more than mastering decoding skills. In an analogy to driving a car decoding would be equivalent to being able to drive – that is, having the functional skills needed for driving – but reading is not only about the functional aspects, but also about obtaining meaning from print. Reading is therefore equivalent to the car driver being able to use the car and navigate it through different surroundings in a strange town. That would mean that the driver has to look for cues and signs that they are on the road they want to be on. If reading is to be effective and efficient the reader has to look for cues and signs that the author has left for them to keep them on track and to follow the story line. A study skills programme in reading is not about basic reading skills, but about reading efficiency. This can be achieved even with readers who have a low level of reading ability. Some reading strategies include skimming, scanning and reading for detail.

- **Scanning** – when scanning, the reader should have some idea of what the text is about so that the key words can stand out more easily. It can be a good idea to highlight the key words in colour or bold print so that the rest of the text will not be distracting.

- **Skimming** – skimming helps the reader obtain the whole picture of the text or passage. It may be necessary to survey the content of the book or browse through the chapters as a way of scanning to get the whole picture.

- **Reading for detail** is used when we have to read short, complicated pieces of text; for example, to identify unfamiliar technical words or complex formulae. This can take time and a different type of approach from that used for scanning and skimming.

## *Writing*

For many students expressive writing can be challenging. Expressive writing incorporates a combination of skills and involves investigation, planning, writing and checking. Some questions learners can ask relating to this are shown below.

Investigation:

- What do I know already about the topic?

- What am I looking for?

- How much information do I need?

- Is this the information I need?

- If not, what else should I be looking for?

- Is there another way of looking at this point?

- Where can I obtain the evidence for other points of view?

Planning:

It is important to understand the question. This in itself is a skill and for some students with particular styles of learning this can be challenging. It is important to obtain practice in interpreting typical essay or examination questions. Agnew et al. (1995) discuss most of the terms that can be used in questioning, some of which can be confusing for the learner. An example of some of these is shown below.

**Analyse** – explore the main ideas of the subject/topic; show why they are important and how they are related.

**Compare** – show the similarities but also point out the differences.

**Discuss** – explore the topic by looking at the advantages and disadvantages – the arguments for and against – and attempt to come to some sort of opinion.

**Explain** – make a topic clear, show the underlying principles, give illustrations and clear examples.

**Summarise** – give a brief account of the main points and attempt to come to some conclusion.

(adapted from Agnew et al., 1995)

A planning framework should focus on the following questions:

- What am I being asked to do?

- What are the key points and key issues?

- Where will I get the information from?

- How long do I have?

Writing:

Some self-questions include:

- Have I kept to the question?

- Does the introduction show clearly what I have written in the essay?

- Have I demonstrated that I have read and understood the topic and question?

- Does the written work flow in a logical and sequential manner?

- Have I linked the paragraphs?

- Does the conclusion show how I have developed the points?

## Teaching study skills

Study skills can be taught as a programme for all students. Heaton and Mitchell (1987) provide a framework for such a programme in their manual *Learning to Learn: A Study Skills Course Book*. This framework includes: time plans, using libraries, reading techniques, spelling, note-taking, understanding the text, selecting and structuring, essay preparation and essay writing, interview techniques, verbal communication, discussion groups, learning from video, TV and films and dealing with examinations.

Similarly, the *Advanced Study Skills* manual by Ostler and Ward (2001) provides a survival guide for students at senior school and college. This book provides a contextualised framework for students to help with the transition from school to college and university.

Another good example of a study skills programme is contained in the *Study Skills Handbook* (Cottrell, 2003). This approach focuses on key factors in learning that can help provide learners with self-knowledge and independence in learning. There are areas of the book that focus on the process of learning and developing writing skills. A major feature of this book is the amount of memory and learning strategies provided to the student but all within a context. These include: reflective learning, effective learning, organising space, managing time, diary-keeping, organisational skills and active learning strategies. One of the interesting aspects of this book is that it can be accessed by high school and college students as well as staff. This promotes the view expressed in this chapter of the importance of empowering students to take responsibility for their own learning.

## Comment on learning strategies

Within the sphere of learning styles the teacher and the student still need to identify appropriate learning strategies. A strategy is essentially a method of ensuring learners' strengths are being used. This means that some strategies will not work for all learners. Strategies are very individual and although there is a vast amount of books on study skills it should not be assumed that a strategy, even one that is seen to be successful, will work for all. Study skills and learning strategies are very individual. But the students will need to be offered a range of possible strategies so that they can select those that are most suited to their learning preferences.

# Insights from students

Since learning strategies are very individual it is important to obtain the views of students. Below are comments from students who have taken important examinations (Lucas, personal correspondence, 2005).

> *The grades that I was expected to get were around borderline pass/fail yet I actually achieved four passes all in the top grades. The reason for the predictions being so low was probably based on the fact that I do not learn well in the classroom environment. The teachers therefore did not realise what I was capable of because my progress in class lessons had not been good.*
>
> *I found my own way of studying. I was motivated because I wanted to go to a good university and to study the course that I wanted. I found it best to spend four hours each day on my own in the library, write my notes out in full and then summarise them until finally I reached the stage when I could fit the large paragraphs that I had summarised on to one line! When all my notes were complete I read them every night in the build up to my exams and the result was that I did a lot better than even I was hoping for. Now I will be able to use this strategy again and I will be even better at using it next time. (Stephen, aged 17 years)*

This is an interesting response because the student realised it was up to him. He took responsibility for his own learning and it paid off. Furthermore, the student had intrinsic motivation. He identified his own goal – a place at a good university – and therefore he was not dependent on external rewards. The incentive came from him. This helped the student identify and appreciate the best way of learning for him. Additionally, having used the strategy, Stephen now considers he will be able to use it again.

Stephen's methods of studying (four hours in the library) contrasts with Ruairdh's, who said that the best way for him was 'to sit down, put on some music, make sure I am completely relaxed and work for twenty to thirty minutes. I would then stay in the same place but do something quite different like reading leisurely for about ten minutes.'

Another student – Mark – found that his best strategy was 'usage'. He uses 'write' and 'check' techniques to learn vocabulary. He said that 'when revising I get bored so do it in small bursts having a small break in the middle. Then I go back to see if the revision has had any effect.'

The above students do seem to be using an auditory type of strategy, which of course is not suitable for all. Rose, aged 17, said that 'I am a very visual person so I remember diagrams and mental images through visual strategies. I know this because I used the example in English literature from the play *Romeo and Juliet* as being like a "lightning bolt". I found it very useful to have a visual image to associate with a scene or play'. Rose has developed visual approaches to understanding and remembering information but again the important point is that she decided on the approach herself and practised using it as she felt comfortable with it.

Bronte said:

> *I find that I only need to be taught an outline of the subject so that I can sort it into some sort of structure in my brain. The only way I can pick up detailed knowledge is to sit down on my own for long periods of time and write out detailed, structured notes with mind maps. I'm very much the kind of person who has to write facts out lots of times to learn them! If I can't see a logical sequence in a subject, I find it very difficult to take on board – it is important to me to see the whole picture before I can start to concentrate on the smaller bits.*

Bronte provides a good example of a learner who uses both analytic, auditory approaches and visual and global approaches. She needs structure, needs to write things out and has to learn through knowing the logical sequence of events. This is an analytic and auditory type of approach, but yet Bronte also needs to use mind maps to see the visual images and to make the connections. Importantly, she also needs to have an overview of the whole picture of what she is studying. This tends to be a global, right-brained type of approach. This emphasises the importance of students themselves deciding on their learning preferences and styles.

The students in this sample were all senior students and had been introduced to study skills throughout school. It was relatively easy for them therefore to identify the most appropriate method for them and experiment with these methods. It is important that students are allowed to do this and given encouragement to find the best style for them. The younger the age this process starts the better. This has been noted by Bertolotto (personal correspondence, 2005) in a study of a class group of 10–11 year olds. Having received input into learning styles and study skills in the form of project work, the young students were then asked to indicate how they learnt best. The responses were very rich in detail and all were able to relate to their learning style.

Two examples of these are shown in Figures 10.1 and 10.2.

There are a number of important points about the above. One key point is that the children have become aware that learning matters. It does not just happen; the learner has to make it happen. One even mentioned the need to 'create a supporting learning environment'. Another made the comment about 'connecting with previous learning'.

The study highlights that children are aware of their learning preferences. This was also found in a study of poetry appreciation among 9–10 year old children (Allwood, 2005). She found that the kinaesthetic learners most preferred the onomatopoeia aspect of poetry and least preferred the alphabet/auditory aspects. The visual learners preferred the shape and form of the poem and also least preferred the alphabet/auditory aspects. Similarly, in a qualitative study by Wright (2005) that looked at the effects of learning styles on writing skills in 8–9 year old children, she found that there was notable development in the skills required for effective writing after helping the children identify their learning style and teaching to that learning style over a period of time.

These studies highlight the view that even young children do have preferences and these preferences can have an impact on class work and performances. Learning styles and study skills, however, need a context to make the information meaningful. A context can help learners understand why they are finding a particular task easy or difficult, and help them take responsibility for controlling their own learning and seeking to find the means of making learning more efficient for them.

It is important to enter into dialogue with children and ask them about their learning preferences. Like all areas, learning styles have to be introduced carefully to the children. Meal (2005) indicated that he ensures this is done in the pre-school period so that young children are aware of how they learn. This helps children begin to take responsibility for their own learning, even at this young age.

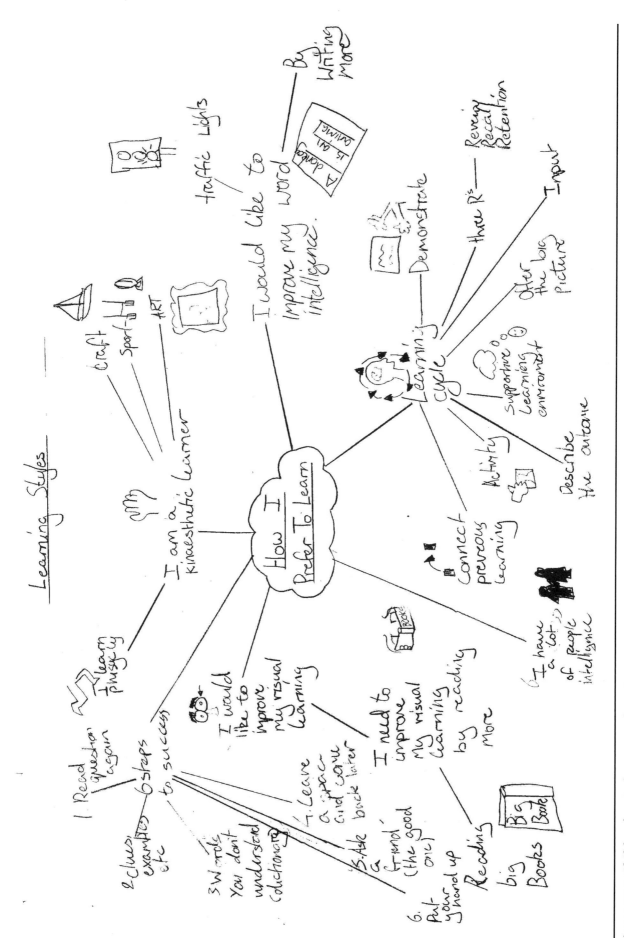

**Figure 10.1 Children's mind maps on learning**

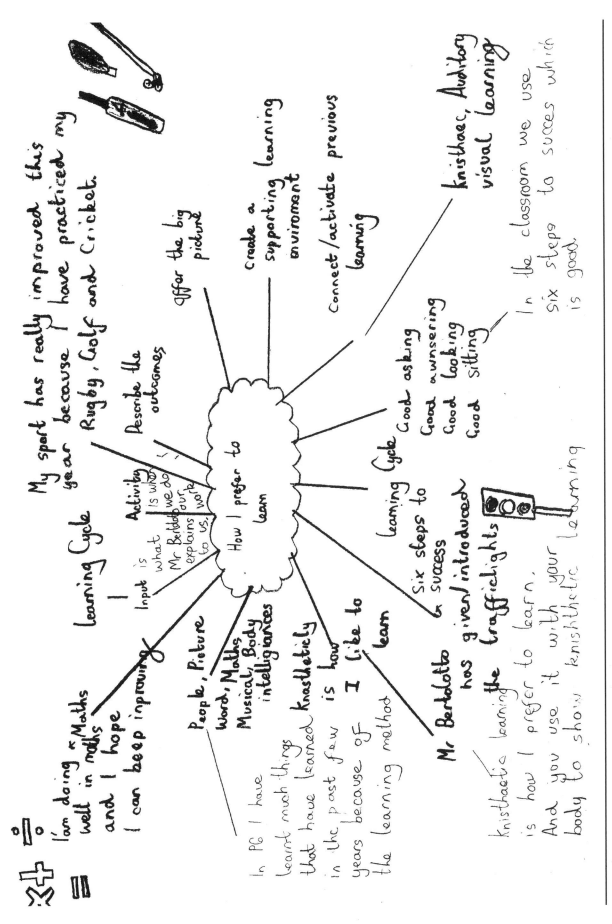

Figure 10.2 Children's mind maps on learning

# Learning about Learning Styles

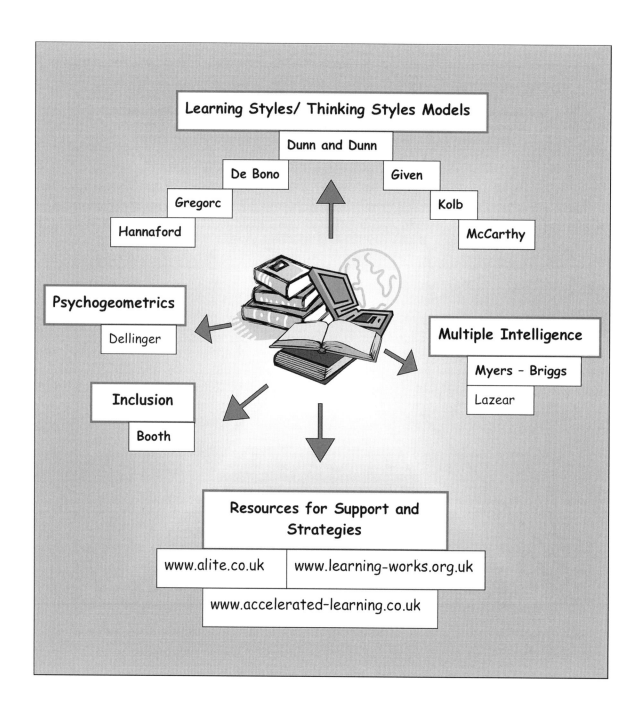

Learning Styles/ Thinking Styles Models

Dunn and Dunn

De Bono

Gregorc

Hannaford

Given

Kolb

McCarthy

Psychogeometrics

Dellinger

Multiple Intelligence

Myers – Briggs

Lazear

Inclusion

Booth

Resources for Support and Strategies

www.alite.co.uk   www.learning-works.org.uk

www.accelerated-learning.co.uk

# Books, Resources and Information

## Books and articles

Anderson, O., Marsh, M. and Harvey, A. (1999) *Learn with the Classics – Using Music to Study Smart at Any Age*. San Francisco, CA: LIND Institute, www.lind-institute.com; also available from the Accelerated Learning Centre, www.accelerated-learning.co.uk

Armstrong, T. (2004) *Multiple Intelligences in the Classroom*. Alexandria, VA: Association for Supervision and Curriculum Development

Buzan, T. (2003) *Brain Child – How Smart Parents Make Smart Kids*. London: Thorsons Press

Caine, R. and Caine, G. (1998) *Unleashing the Power of Perceptual Change*. Alexandria, VA: Association for Supervision and Curriculum Development

Campbell, D. (1997) *The Mozart Effect*. New York: Avon Books, available at www.accelerated-learning.co.uk

Carnell, E. and Lodge, C. (2002) *Supporting Effective Learning*. London: Paul Chapman Publishing

Cooke, G. and Brough, M. (2002) *Learning Toolkit*, Vols 1 and 2. Marlborough: Fil Came, Learning Works, www.learning-works.org.uk

De Bono, E. (1995) *Six Thinking Hats*. Boston, MA: Little Brown and Co.

Dellinger, S. (1989) *Psychometrics: How to Use Geometric Psychology to Influence People*. Englewood Cliffs, NJ: Prentice Hall

Dunn, R. and Dunn, K. (1993) *Teaching Secondary Students Through Their Individual Learning Styles*. Boston, MA: Allyn & Bacon

Dunn, R. and Griggs, S.A. (1995) *Multiculturalism and Learning Style*. Westport, CT: Praeger

Ginnis, P. (2002) *The Teacher's Toolkit: Raise Classroom Achievement with Strategies for Every Learner*. Carmarthen: Crown House Publishing, www.crownhouse.co.uk

Given, B.K. (2002) *Teaching to the Brain's Natural Learning System*. Alexandria, VA: Association for Supervision and Curriculum Development

Gregorc, A. (1996) *Inside Styles – Beyond the Basics, Questions and Answers on Style*. Columbia, CT: Gregorc Assoc. Inc., www.gregorc.com/

Gregorc, D.F. (1997) *Relating with Style*. Columbia, CT: Gregorc Assoc. Inc.

Hannaford, C. (1995) *Smart Moves – Why Learning Is Not All in Your Head*. Arlington, VA: Great Ocean Publishers

Hannaford, C. (1997) *The Dominance Factor – How Knowing Your Dominant Eye, Ear, Brain, Hand and Foot Can Improve Your Learning*. Arlington, VA: Great Ocean Publishers

Healy, J. (1994) *Your Child's Growing Mind*. New York: Doubleday

Healy, J. (1998) *Failure to Connect – How Computers Affect Our Children's Minds – for Better or Worse*. New York: Simon and Schuster

Jonassen, D.H. and Grabowski, B.L. (1993) *Handbook of Individual Differences, Learning and Instruction*. Hillsdale, NJ: Lawrence Erlbaum Associates

Kolb, A. and Kolb, D.A. (2001) *Experiential Learning Theory Bibliography 1971–2001*. Boston, MA: McBer

Kolb, D.A. (1976) *The Learning Style Inventory: Technical Manual*. Boston, MA: McBer

Kolb, D.A. (1984) *Experiential Learning*. Englewood Cliffs, NJ: Prentice Hall

Lawrence, G. (1993) *People Types and Tiger Stripes*. Gainsville, FL: Center for Applications of Psychological Type, Inc., www.myersbriggs.org/

Lazear, D. (2004a) *Outsmart Yourself! 16 Proven Strategies for Becoming Smarter than You Think You Are*. David Lazear Products, www.davidlazear.com

Lazear, D. (2004b) *Multiple Intelligence Approaches to Assessment: Solving the Assessment Conundrum*. Carmarthen: Crown House Publishing

McCarthy, B. (1987) *The 4 Mat System – Teaching to Learning Styles with Right/Left Mode Techniques*. Barrington, IL: Excel Inc.

MacGilchrist, B., Myers, K. and Reed, J. (2004) *The Intelligent School* (2nd edn). London: Sage Publications

North, V. with Buzan, T. (2001) *Get Ahead* (5th edn). Dorset: B.C. Books

Ostler, C. and Ward, F. (2001) *Advanced Study Skills* (reprinted 2004). Outwood, Wakefield: SEN Marketing

Prashnig, B. (2004) *The Power of Diversity*. Auckland, New Zealand: Creative Learning Company, www.creativelearningcentre.com/products.asp?page=PODBOK

Riding, R. (2002) *School Learning and Cognitive Style*. London: David Fulton

Riding, R. and Rayner, S. (1998) *Cognitive Style and Learning Strategies*. London: David Fulton

Sprenger, M. (2003) *Differentiation Through Learning Styles and Memory*. Thousand Oaks, CA: Corwin Press

Sternberg, R. (1997) *Thinking Styles*. Cambridge: Cambridge University Press

Walker Tileston, D. (2005) *Ten Best Teaching Practices. How Brain Research, Learning Styles, and Standards Define Teaching Competencies* (2nd edn). Thousand Oaks, CA: Corwin Press

## Resources

Kolb's Experiential Learning Style Model
www.infed.org/biblio/b-explrn.htm

Myers Briggs Type Indicator
www.myersbriggs.org/
www.capt.org/the_mbti_instrument/Overview.cfm

Using Multiple Intelligences
http://4teachers.org/projectbased/intell.shtml
see www.creativelearningcentre.com/

## Other learning styles links

Learning Styles Site at Indiana State University
www-isu.indstate.edu/ctl/styles/articles.html

Holland's Personality Types and career choices
www.careerkey.org/english/you/hollands_home.html

University of Minnesota Duluth web page on learning and learning styles
Theory into Practice (TIP) database
http://tip.psychology.org/index.html

Dr Anthony F. Gregorc
www.gregorc.com/

Gregorc's Learning Style
www.indiana.edu/~w505a/learningstyles.html

Anatomy atlas of the whole brain
www.med.harvard.edu/AANLIB/

Information about Brain Gym®
www.learning-solutions.co.uk/brain-gym.php
www.thebrainstore.com
www.braingym.org

The main site for circle-time – Jenny Mosley
www.circle-time.co.uk

Details of Alistair Smith's work
www.alite.co.uk

Fun Track Learning Centre, Perth, Western Australia
Mandy Appleyard, Educational Consultant
Unit 2, 590 Stirling Highway, Mosman Park WA 6012
PO Box 134 Mosman Park WA 6912
www.funtrack.com.au

Creative Learning Company, New Zealand
www.creativelearningcentre.com

Mindroom – Organisation for learning difficulties including ADHD
www.mindroom.org

Loretta Giorcelli's website – highly recommended international consultant
www.doctorg.org

Accelerated learning sites
www.accelerated-learning.co.uk
www.alcenter.com

Red Rose School, 28-30 North Promenade
St Annes on Sea, Lancashire FY8 2NQ, England – school designed to cater for individual
learning styles
www.redroseschool.co.uk

REACH Learning Center, 121A-123 East 15th Street
North Vancouver, B.C. Canada, V7M 1R7 www.reachlearningcenter.com
REACH provides multisensory lessons designed specifically for each student prior to each
lesson. Reports are given that outline specifically the skills that the student is learning.
Dedicated to parent education and meeting individual learning needs.
REACH Directors:
Corey Zylstra zylstra@reachlearningcenter.com
Shannon Green green@reachlearningcenter.com

Teachers Network
www.teachnet.org

Dana Foundation – provides information about the brain and current brain research
www.dana.org

# Book Overview

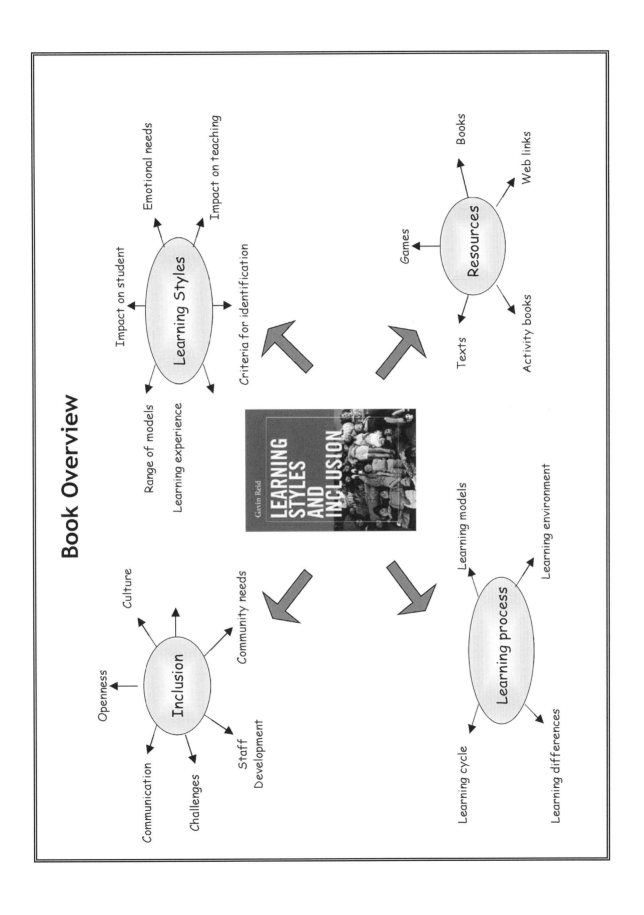

Learning Styles
- Emotional needs
- Impact on teaching
- Impact on student
- Criteria for identification
- Range of models
- Learning experience

Resources
- Books
- Web links
- Games
- Activity books
- Texts

Inclusion
- Culture
- Community needs
- Openness
- Communication
- Challenges
- Staff Development

Learning process
- Learning models
- Learning environment
- Learning cycle
- Learning differences

Gavin Reid
LEARNING STYLES AND INCLUSION

# GLOSSARY

**ADHD:** attention deficit hyperactivity disorders. Characterised by inattention, lack of control over learning and attention and impulsive behaviour.

**Analytic:** term used to describe a learning or processing style. Usually left-hemisphere style that indicates a preference for learning details and facts.

**Automaticity:** when a learned skill becomes automatic, e.g. riding a bicycle, swimming.

**Behaviourism:** name given to models of learning that usually promote reward and reinforcement, or punishment and withdrawal of privileges to provide the desired or target behaviour.

**Cognition:** processes involved in thinking and learning.

**Cognitive modifiability:** suggests that learning capacity can be increased irrespective of the ability or difficulties experienced by the learner, usually by promoting certain types of learning behaviours or through rehearsal and targeting the most appropriate behaviours. This is the cornerstone of Feuerstein's theory of Instrumental Enrichment (see Chapter 9).

**Constructivism:** emphasises the construction of learning, often in stages such as in Piaget's theory (see Chapter 1), over time. Indicates that learning is related to development.

**DCD:** developmental co-ordination disorders such as dyspraxia. Indicates difficulty with co-ordination and movement. Can affect handwriting and gross motor skills such as those used in most active sports.

**Dynamic assessment:** sometimes referred to as **assisted assessment**. Indicates that the learner is supported through assessment and notes are made of the type of assistance that eventually provides the correct response. Makes assessment a learning and teaching process and usually takes place over a period of time.

**Dyscalculia:** difficulties with number computation and concepts, may include difficulty in remembering number bonds and number sequences.

**Dyslexia:** difficulty with processing some forms of information, usually print based. Associated difficulties can include poor memory, organisation, directional confusion, processing speed and written expression.

**Global:** term used to describe holistic processing style, usually visual and holistic. Often associated with right-hemisphere processing.

**Learned helplessness:** phrase used to describe learners who perceive themselves as failing in a task because of previous failing experiences. Often results in demotivation.

**Metacognition:** awareness of the learning process, being able to use learning skills efficiently.

**Mozart effect:** expression used to describe the calming, learning and therapeutic powers of music, particularly music composed by Mozart.

**Multiple intelligences:** term developed by Howard Gardner to describe the range of attributes an individual can use in learning. Gardner's model of multiple intelligences identified eight intelligences. Indicated a shift from traditional perspectives on intelligence.

**Overlearning:** term used to describe the process of presenting the same information in a variety of ways. Often used for learners with dyslexia, can help to develop automaticity (see **automaticity** above).

**Reciprocal teaching:** method of teaching that involves question-and-response interaction between teacher and learner to promote and develop the learner's understanding of a subject. Can be associated with **dynamic assessment** (see above).

**Scaffolding:** links between different areas learning new material or new skills, helps to access new learning.

**Scotopic sensitivity:** indicates a sensitivity to certain light patterns and to glare. Print can become distorted; can be associated with migraine headaches and some allergies.

**Working memory:** the processing of information in short-term memory.

**Zone of Proximal Development:** comfort zone for new learning to take place, describes learner's current knowledge and implies that the learner requires sufficient background understanding to enable new learning to take place.

# References

Agnew, M., Barlow, S., Pascal, L. and Skidmore, S. (1995) *Get Better Grades – Cool Study Skills*. London: Piccadilly Press

Alexander, R. (2000) *Culture and Pedagogy: International Comparisons in Primary Education*. Oxford: Blackwell

Allwood, S. (2005) *The Impact of Learning Styles in Creative Writing*. Unpublished BEd Dissertation. University of Edinburgh, Scotland

Anderson, O., Marsh, M. and Harvey, A. (1999) *Learn with the Classics, Using Music to Study Smart at Any Age*. San Francisco, CA: LIND Institute

Andrade, A. (1999) *The Thinking Classroom, Based on the Collective Research and Ideas of the Cognitive Skills Group*, Harvard Project Zero, USA

Armstrong, T. (2004) *Multiple Intelligences in the Classroom*. Alexandria, VA: Association for Supervision and Curriculum Development

Atkinson, M. (2005) Opening address, Gateshead Inclusion Conference 3, Communication in Focus, 15 April, Gateshead Council, UK

Ausubel, D.P. (1968) *Educational Psychology, A Cognitive View*. New York: Holt, Rinehart and Winston

Bandura, A. (1977) *Social Learning Theory*. Englewood Cliffs, NJ: Prentice Hall

Bell, N. (1991) *Visualizing and Verbalizing for Language Comprehension and Thinking*. Paso Robles, CA: Academy of Reading Publications

Bennett, C. (1986) *Comprehensive Multicultural Education, Theory and Practice*. Boston, MA: Allyn & Bacon

Bloom, B.S. (ed.) (1956) *Taxonomy of Educational Objectives: The Classification of Educational Goals: Handbook I, Cognitive Domain*. New York; Toronto: Longmans, Green

Booth, T., Ainscow, M., Black-Hawkins, K., Vaughn, M. and Shaw, L. (2000) *Index for Inclusion: Developing Learning and Participation in Schools*. Bristol: Centre for Studies in Inclusive Education (CSIE)

Bransford, J.D., Brown, A.L. and Cocking, R.R. (eds) (2000) *How People Learn; Brain, Mind, Experience and School*. Commission on Behavioural and Social Sciences and Education, National Research Council. Washington, DC: National Academy Press

Brechin, C. (2004) *Self-knowledge in Learning Can Provide Emotional Support for Dyslexic Children. A School-based Research Study*. Unpublished MEd Dissertation, University of Edinburgh, Scotland

Breslin, A. (2005) Personal correspondence

Bronfenbrenner, U. (1979) *The Ecology of Human Development*. Cambridge, MA: Harvard University Press

Brown, A.L. and Campione, J.C. (1994) 'Guided discovery in a community of learners', in K. McGilly (ed.) *Classroom Lessons; Integrating Cognitive Theory and Classroom Practice*, pp229–70. Cambridge MA: MIT Press

Bruner, J.S. (1965) *The Process of Education*. Cambridge, MA: Harvard University Press

Burden, R.L. (1998) 'Assessing children's perceptions of themselves as learners and problem solvers: the construction of the Myself-As-Learner Scale (MALS)', *School Psychology International* 19(4), 291–305

Burden, R.L. (2000) *The Myself-As-Learner Scale (MALS)*. Windsor: NFER-Nelson

Burden, R.L. (2002) *A Cognitive Approach to Dyslexia: Learning Styles and Thinking Skills*. Windsor: NFER-Nelson

Burden, R.L. and Fraser, B.J. (1993) 'The use of classroom environment assessments in school psychology: a British perspective', *Psychology in the Schools*, 30, 232–40

Butterworth, B. and Yeo, D (2004) *Dyscalculia Guidance; Helping Pupils with Specific Learning Difficulties in Maths*. London: NFER/Nelson with David Fulton Publishers

Buzan, T. (2003) *The Mind Map Book: Radiant Thinking, the Major Evolution in Human Thought* (3rd edn). London: BBC Books

Caine, R. and Caine, G. (1998) *Unleashing the Power of Perceptual Change*. Alexandria, VA: Association for Supervision and Curriculum Development

Came, F. and Cooke, G. (2001) *Memory Trainers, Techniques, Games and Systems to Teach and Improve Memory Skills*. Marlborough: Learning Works International

Came, F., Cooke, G. and Brough, M. (2002a) *Learning Toolkit Volume 1 Personal Learning*. Marlborough: Learning Works International

Came, F., Cooke, G. and Brough, M. (2002b) *Learning Toolkit Volume 2 Learning Tools*. Marlborough: Learning Works International

Camilleri, A. (1997) 'Introducing learner autonomy in initial teacher training', in H. Holec and I. Huttunen (eds) *Learner Autonomy in Modern Languages*. Strasbourg: Council of Europe

Camilleri, A. (1999) *Learner Autonomy in Modern Languages; Finding your Bearing and Pick your Way*. Faculty of Education, University of Malta (www.letmelearn.org/research/camilleri.html)

Campbell, D. (1997) *The Mozart Effect*. New York: Avon Books (available at www.accelerated-learning.co.uk)

Carnell, E. and Lodge, C. (2002) *Supporting Effective Learning*. London: Paul Chapman Publishing

Coffield, F. (2005) 'Kinesthetic nonsense', *Times Educational Supplement*, 14 January, p28

Coffield, F., Moseley, D., Hall, E. and Ecclestone, K. (2004) 'Should we be using learning styles? What the research has to say to practice'. Learning and Skills Research Centre, Learning and Skills Development Agency, London (www.LSRC.ac.uk)

Cooke, G., Came, F. and Brough, B. (2002) *Learning Styles: A New Look at Differentiation*. Marlborough: Learning Works International

Cottrell, S. (2003) *The Study Skills Handbook* (2nd edn). Hampshire: Palgrave Macmillan

Covington, M.E. (1992) *Making the Grade*. Cambridge: Cambridge University Press

Cudd, E.T. and Roberts, L.L. (1994) 'A scaffolding technique to develop sentence sense and vocabulary', *The Reading Teacher*, 47(4), 346–9

Curry, L. (1987) *Integrating Concepts of Cognitive or Learning Style: A Review with Attention to Psychometric Standards*. Ottawa: Canadian College of Health Service Executives

De Bono, E. (1995) *Six Thinking Hats*. Boston, MA: Little Brown and Co.

Dellinger, S. (1989) *Psychometrics: How to Use Geometric Psychology to Influence People*. Englewood Cliffs, NJ: Prentice Hall

Denicolo, P. and Pope, M. (2001) *Transformational Professional Practice: Personal Construct Approaches to Education and Research*. London: Whurr Publications

Dennison, G.E. and Dennison, P.E. (2000) *Educational Kinesiology Brain Organisation Profiles. Teachers' Training Manual* (3rd edn). Glendale, CA: Educ. Kinesthetics

Dennison, P.E. and Hargrove, G. (1985) *Personalized Whole Brain Integration*. Glendale, CA: Educ. Kinesthetics

Department for Education and Employment (DfEE) (2000) *Research into Teacher Effectiveness*. London: DfEE

Department for Education and Skills (DfES) (2002) *Key Stage 3 National Strategy: Guidance and Curriculum Standards. Learning Styles and Writing in History, Science, Modern Languages, Physical Education, Mathematics and English*. London: DfES

Deschler, D. and Schumaker, J.B. (1987) 'An instructional manual for teaching students how to learn', in J.L. Graden, J.E. Zins and M.J. Curtis (eds) *Alternative Educational Delivery Systems: Enhancing Instructional Aspects for all Students*. University of Kansas, Institute for Research in Learning Difficulties

Diamond, M. and Hopson, J. (1989) *Magic Trees of the Mind.* New York: Dutton

Diniz, F.A. (2002) *Culture and Equity. Audio for Difficulties in Literacy Development* (E801 course materials). Buckingham: Open University Press

Dockrell, J. and McShane, J. (1993) *Children's Learning Difficulties – A Cognitive Approach.* Oxford: Blackwell

Dunn, R. (1997) 'The goals and track record of multicultural education', *Educational Leadership,* 54(7), 74–7

Dunn, R. and Dunn, K. (1993) *Teaching Secondary Students through Their Individual Learning Styles.* Boston, MA: Allyn & Bacon

Dunn, R. and Griggs, S. (1995) *Multiculturalism and Learning Style.* Westport, CT: Praeger

Dunn, R., Dunn, K. and Price, G.E. (1975, 1979, 1985, 1987, 1989) *Learning Styles Inventory.* Lawrence, KA: Price Systems, Inc.

Dweck, C.S. and Licht, B.G. (1980) 'Learned helplessness and intellectual achievement', in J. Garber and M.E.P. Seligman (eds) *Human Helplessness: Theory and Applications.* New York: Academic Press

Eadon, H. (2004) *Dyslexia and Drama.* London: David Fulton

Edelman, G.M. (1992) *Bright Air, Brilliant Fire. On the Matter of the Mind.* New York: Basic Books

EFECOT (1999) *Travelling on Together.* Brussels: EFECOT (www.efecot.net)

Felder, R. (1993) 'Reaching the second tier: learning and teaching styles in college science education', *J. College Science Teaching,* 23(5), 286–90

Feuerstein, R. (1979) *The Dynamic Assessment of Retarded Performers: The Learning Potential Assessment Device, Theory, Instruments and Techniques.* Baltimore, MD: University Park Press

Feuerstein, R., Rand, Y., Hoffman, M. and Miller, R. (1980) *Instrumental Enrichment: An Intervention Programme for Cognitive Modifiability.* Baltimore, MD: University Park Press

Fitts, P.M. and Posner, M.I. (1967) *Human Performance.* Belmont, CA: Brooks-Cole

Flavell, J.H. (1976) 'Metacognitive aspects of problem solving', in L.B. Resnick (ed.) *The Nature of Intelligence.* Hillsdale, NJ: Lawrence Erlbaum Associates

Flavell, J.H. and Wellman, H.M. (1977) 'Metamemory', in R.V. Kail and J.W. Hagen (eds) *Perspectives on the Development of Memory and Cognition.* Hillsdale, NJ: Lawrence Erlbaum Associates

Florian, L. (2005) 'Inclusion, special needs and the search for new understandings', *Support for Learning,* 20(2), 96–8

Frederickson, N. and Cline, T. (2002) *Special Educational Needs, Inclusion and Diversity, a Text Book.* Buckingham: Open University Press

Gardner, H. (1983) *Frames of Mind. The Theory of Multiple Intelligences.* New York: Harper and Row

Gardner, H. (1985) *Frames of Mind.* New York: Basic Books

Gardner, H. (1991) *The Unschooled Mind: How Children Think and How Schools Should Teach.* New York: Basic Books

Gardner, H. (1999) *The Disciplined Mind.* London: Simon and Schuster

Geuze, R.H., Jongmans, M.J., Schoemaker, M.M. and Smits-Engelsman, B.C. (2001) 'Clinical and research diagnostic criteria for developmental coordination disorder: A review and discussion', *Human Movement Science,* 20(12), 7–47

Ginnis, P. (2002) *The Teacher's Toolkit: Raising Classroom Achievement with Strategies for Every Classroom.* Carmarthen: Crown House Publishing

Giorcelli, L.R. (1995) *An Impulse to Soar: Sanitisation, Silencing and Special Education.* The Des English Memorial Lecture. Australian Association of Special Education Conference, Darwin. Reproduced in SPELD Celebration of Learning Styles conference proceedings, 1996 conference. Christchurch, New Zealand

Giorcelli, L.R. (1999) 'Inclusion and other factors affecting teacher attitudes to literacy programs for students with special needs', in A.J. Watson and L.R. Giorcelli (eds) *Accepting the Literacy Challenge.* Gosford, Australia: Scholastic Publications

Given, B.K. (1996) 'The potential of learning styles', in G. Reid (ed.) *Dimensions of Dyslexia. Vol. 2: Literacy, Language and Learning.* Edinburgh: Moray House Publications

Given, B.K. (1998) 'Psychological and neurobiological support for learning-style instruction. Why it works', *National Forum of Applied Educational Research Journal*, 11(1), 10–15

Given, B.K. (2002) *Teaching to the Brain's Natural Learning System*. Alexandria, VA: Association for Supervision and Curriculum Development

Given, B.K. and Reid, G. (1999) *Learning Styles: A Guide for Teachers and Parents*. St Anne's-on-Sea, Lancashire: Red Rose Publications

Grasha, A. (1996) *Teaching with Style*. Pittsburgh, PA: Alliance Publishers

Graziano, A.B., Peterson, M. and Shaw, G.L. (1999) 'Enhanced learning of proportional math through music training and spatial–temporal training', *Neurological Research*, 21, March, 139–52

Green, S. (2005) *Personal Correspondence* REACH Learning Center, Vancouver, B.C. Canada

Gregorc, A.F. (1985) *Inside Styles: Beyond the Basics*. Columbia, CT: Gregorc Assoc. Inc.

Gregorc, D.F. (1997) *Relating with Style*. Columbia, CT: Gregorc Assoc. Inc.

Guild, P.B. (2001) *Diversity, Learning Style and Culture*. Seattle, WA: New Horizons for Learning (www.newhorizons.org)

Hannaford, C. (1995) *Smart Moves. Why Learning Is Not All in Your Head*. Arlington, VA: Great Ocean Publishers

Hannaford, C. (1997) *The Dominance Factor. How Knowing Your Dominant Eye, Ear, Brain, Hand and Foot Can Improve Your Learning*. Arlington, VA: Great Ocean Publishers

Hart, S., Dixon, A., Drummond., M.J. and McIntyre, D. (2004) *Learning without Limits*. Buckingham: Open University Press

Healy, J. (1992) *How to Have Intelligent and Creative Conversations with Your Kids*. New York: Doubleday

Healy, J. (1994) *Your Child's Growing Mind: A Practical Guide to Brain Development and Learning from Birth to Adolescence*. New York: Doubleday

Heaton, P. and Mitchell, G. (1987) *Learning to Learn: A Study Skills Course Book*. Bath: Better Books

Henderson, A., Came, F. and Brough, M. (2003) *Working with Dyscalculia; Recognising Dyscalculia; Overcoming Barriers in Maths*. Marlborough: Learning Works (www.learning-works.org.uk)

Hopper, C. (2003) *Practicing College Study Skills: Strategies for Success* (3rd edn). Boston, MA: Houghton Mifflin Company

Irlen, H.L. (1991) *Reading by the Colors: Overcoming Dyslexia and Other Reading Disabilities through the Irlen Method*. New York: Avebury Publishing

Jackson, C. (2002) *Jackson's Learning Styles Profiler* (LSP) (available at www.psi-press.co.uk)

Johnston, C.A. (1996) *Unlocking The Will To Learn*. Thousand Oaks, CA: Corwin Press

Johnston, C.A. (1998) *Let Me Learn*. Thousand Oaks, CA: Corwin Press

Jonassen, D.H. and Grabowski, B.L. (1993) *Handbook of Individual Differences, Learning and Instruction*. Hillsdale, NJ: Lawrence Erlbaum Associates

Jones, N. (2005) 'Including children with specific learning difficulties', in N. Jones (ed.) *Developing School Provision for Children with Dyspraxia; A Practical Guide*. London: Sage Publications

Jordan, E. (2001) 'Interrupted learning: The traveller paradigm', *Support for Learning*, 16(3), 128–34

Keefe, J.W. (1987) *Learning Style – Theory and Practice*. Reston, VA: National Association of Secondary School Principals

Keefe, J.W. (1991) *Learning Style: Cognitive and Thinking Skills*. Reston, VA: National Association of Secondary School Principals

Kline, P. (1988) *The Everyday Genius, Restoring Children's Natural Joy of Learning – and Yours Too*. Arlington, VA: Great Ocean Publishers

Kolb, A. and Kolb, D.A. (2001) *Experiential Learning Theory Bibliography 1971–2001*. Boston, MA: McBer

Kolb, D.A. (1976) *The Learning Style Inventory: Technical Manual*, Boston, MA: McBer

Kolb, D.A. (1984a) *Learning Style Inventory Technical Manual*. Boston, MA: McBer

Kolb, D.A. (1984b) *Experiential Learning*. Englewood Cliffs, NJ: Prentice Hall

Kozulin, A. and Rand, Y. (eds) (2000) *Experience of Mediated Learning: An Impact of Feuerstein's Theory in Education and Psychology*. Oxford: Pergamon

Landon, J. (2001) 'Inclusion and dyslexia: The exclusion of bilingual learners?', in L. Peer and G. Reid (eds) *Dyslexia – Successful Inclusion in Secondary School*. London: David Fulton

Lannen, S. (2002) personal correspondence

Lannen, C., Lannen, S. and Reid, G. (2004) 'Parents' attitudes to provision and support for children with specific learning difficulties', Report for European Commission Grundtvig 2 Project, Dyslexia – Parents and Teachers Collaboration (DYPATEC). Project Number G2-04-1-K-L-195, European Commission, Brussels

Lawrence, G. (1993) *People Types and Tiger Stripes* (3rd edn). Gainsville, FL: Center for Applications of Psychological Type, Inc.

Lazear, D. (1994) *Multiple Intelligences Approaches to Assessment*. Tucson, AR: Zephyr Press

Lazear, D. (1999) *Eight Ways of Knowing: Teaching for Multiple Intelligences* (3rd edn). Arlington Heights, IL: Skylight Professional Development

Lazear, D. (2004a) *Outsmart Yourself! 16 Proven Strategies for Becoming Smarter than You Think You Are.* David Lazear Products (www.davidlazear.com)

Lazear, D. (2004b) *Multiple Intelligence Approaches to Assessment; Solving the Assessment Conundrum.* Carmarthen: Crown House Publishing

Lidz, C.S. (ed.) (1987) *Dynamic Assessment*. New York: Guilford Press

Lindsey, L., Perkins, J. and Betts, A. (2004) 'Our successful journey to inclusion'. Summer workshop presentation, West Feliciana Parish Schools, Louisiana (http://www.ed.gov/teachers/how/tools/initiative/summerworkshop/westfeliciana/index.html)

McBeath, J. and Mortimore, P. (eds) (2001) *Improving School Effectiveness*. Buckingham: Open University Press

McCarthy, B. (1987) *The 4 Mat System – Teaching to Learning Styles with Right/Left Mode Techniques.* Barrington, IL: Excel Inc.

MacGilchrist, B., Myers, K. and Reed, J. (2004) *The Intelligent School* (2nd edn). London: Sage Publications

Macintyre, C. and Deponio, P. (2003) *Identifying and Supporting Children with Specific Learning Difficulties; Looking Beyond the Label to Assess the Whole Child.* London: RoutledgeFalmer

McNamara, S. and Moreton, G. (1997) *Understanding Differentiation*. London: David Fulton

Marland, M. (1981) 'Information skills in the secondary curriculum', *Schools Council Curriculum Bulletin*, 9. London: Methuen

Mathews, M. (1993) 'Can children be helped by applied kinesiology?'. Paper presented at 5th European Conference in Neuro-Developmental Delay in Children with Specific Learning Difficulties, Chester

Meal, S. (2005) Personal interview. Davidson's Mains Primary School, Edinburgh

Mittler, P. (2000) *Working Towards Inclusive Education: Social Contexts*. London: David Fulton

Monroe, W.S. (1924) *Training in the Technique of Study*, Bulletin 20, Bureau of Educational Research, University of Illinois

Mortimore, T. (2003) *Dyslexia and Learning Styles: A Practitioner's Handbook.* London: Whurr Publications

Mosston, M. and Ashworth, S. (1990) *The Spectrum of Teaching Styles from Command to Discovery.* White Plains, NY: Longman

Nicolson, R. and Fawcett, A. (2004) 'Climbing the reading mountain: Learning from the science of learning', in G. Reid and A. Fawcett (eds) *Dyslexia in Context; Research, Policy and Practice.* London: Whurr Publications

Nisbet, J. and Shucksmith, J. (1986) *Learning Strategies*. London: Routledge Education

North, V. with Buzan, T. (2001) *Get Ahead; Mind Map® Your Way to Success* (5th edn). Dorset: B.C. Books

Norwich, B., Goodchild, L. and Lloyd, S. (2001) 'Some aspects of the inclusion index in operation', *Support for Learning*, 16(4), 156–61

Ostler, C. and Ward, F. (2001) *Advanced Study Skills*. Outwood, Wakefield: SEN Marketing

Palincsar, A. and Brown, A. (1984) 'Reciprocal teaching of comprehension fostering and comprehension monitoring activities', *Cognition and Instruction*, 1(2), 117–75

Piaget, J. (1954) *The Construction of Reality in the Child*. New York: Basic Books

Piaget, J. (1970) *The Science of Education and the Psychology of the Child*. New York: Viking Press

Piers, E.V. and Harris, D. (1964) 'Age and other correlates of self-concept in children', *Journal of Educational Psychology*, 55, 91–5

Portwood, M. (2004) 'Dyspraxia', in A. Lewis and B. Norwich (eds) *Special Teaching for Special Children? Pedagogies for Inclusion*. Buckingham: OU Press/McGraw-Hill Education

Posch, L. (2004) *Culture Shock:* The Psychology of Intercultural Encounters, Zwettl, WLV and sbz Waldviertler Lehrmittelerlag and Schulbedarfszentrum, Austria: Graz.

Prashnig, B. (2004) *The Power Of Diversity*. Auckland, New Zealand: Creative Learning Company

Qualifications and Curriculum Authority (2000) *The General Statement on Inclusion. Curriculum 2000*. London: QCA

Reid, G. (1996) 'The other side of dyslexia', in G. Reid (ed.) *Dimensions of Dyslexia Vol.2 Literacy, Language and Learning*. Edinburgh: Moray House Publications

Reid, G. (2003) *Dyslexia: A Practitioner's Handbook* (3rd edn). Chichester: John Wiley and Sons

Reid, G. (2004) 'Dyslexia', in A. Lewis and B. Norwich (eds) *Special Teaching for Special Children? Pedagogies for Inclusion*. Buckingham: Open University Press

Reid, G. (2005a) 'The spectrum of specific learning difficulties', in N. Jones (ed.) *Developing School Provision for Children with Dyspraxia; A Practical Guide*. London: Sage Publications

Reid, G. (2005b) *Dyslexia and Inclusion: Classroom Approaches for Assessment, Teaching and Learning*. London: David Fulton/NASEN

Reid, G. and Kirk, J. (2001) *Dyslexia in Adults: Education and Employment*. Chichester: John Wiley and Sons

Reid, G. and Strnadova, I. (2004) 'The development of teacher and student measures for identifying learning styles'. Pilot research study, University of Edinburgh in collaboration with Charles University, Prague

Remedial Education for Adults and Children (REACH) (2005) Personal correspondence, North Vancouver, Canada

Renzulli, J.S., Leppien, J.H. and Hays, T.S. (2000) (foreword by Carol A. Tomlinson). Mansfield Center, CT: Creative Learning Press, Inc. (www.creativelearningpress.com/)

Richards, R.G. (1993) *LEARN: Playful Techniques to Accelerate Learning*. Tucson, AR: Zephyr Press

Riddell, S. (2002) *Policy and Practice in Education: (5) Special Educational Needs*. Edinburgh: Dunedin Academic Press

Riding, R. (2002) *School Learning and Cognitive Style*. London: David Fulton

Riding, R. and Cheema, L. (1991) 'Cognitive styles – an overview and integration', *Educational Psychology*, 11(3-4), 193–215

Riding, R. and Rayner, S. (1998) *Cognitive Styles and Learning Strategies: Understanding Style Difference in Learning and Behaviour*. London: David Fulton

Rose, R. (1998) 'The curriculum: A vehicle for inclusion or a lever for exclusion?', in C. Tulstone, L. Florian and R. Rose (eds) *Promoting Inclusive Practice*. London: Routledge

Schneider, E. and Crombie, M. (2003) *Dyslexia and Foreign Language Learning*. London: David Fulton

Scottish Executive Education Department (SEED) (2002) *The Standard for Chartered Teachers*. Scottish Executive, Edinburgh (www.scotland.gov.uk/library5/education/sfct-00.asp)

Seidel, L.E. and England, E.M. (1999) 'Gregorc's cognitive styles: College students' preferences for teaching methods and testing techniques', *Perceptual and Motor Skills*, 83(3), 859–75

Senge, P.M. (2000) *The Fifth Discipline: The Art and Practice of the Learning Organisation*. London: Century Business

Setley, S. (1995) *Taming the Dragons: Real Help for Real School Problems*. Higganum: Starfish Publishing Company (starfishpc@aol.com)

Shiel, G. (2002) 'The performance of Irish students in reading literacy in the Programme for International Student Assessment (PISA)', *Irish Journal of Education*, 33, 7–30

Simpson, M. and Ure, J. (1993) *What's the Difference? A Study of Differentiation in Scottish Secondary Schools*. Aberdeen: Northern College

Smiley, P.A. and Dweck, C.S. (1994) 'Individual differences in achievement goals among young children', *Child Development*, 65, 1723–43

Smith, A. (1998) *Accelerated Learning in Practice: Brain-based Methods for Accelerating Motivation and Achievement*. Stafford: Network Educational Press

Smith, A. and Call, N. (2000) *The Alps Approach*. Stafford: Network Educational Press

Smith. A., Lovatt, M. and Wise, D. (2003) *Accelerated Learning*. Stafford: Network Educational Press

Snider, V.E. (1992) 'Learning styles and learning to read: A critique', *Remedial and Special Education*, 13, 6–18

Sprenger, M. (2003) *Differentiation Through Learning Styles and Memory*. Thousand Oaks, CA: Corwin Press

Stahl, S. (1999) 'Different strokes for different folks? A critique of learning styles', *American Educator*, 23(3), 27–31

Stephenson, E. (2000) *Children with Motor Learning Difficulties. A Guide for Parents and Teachers*. Aberdeen: Occupational Therapy Department, Royal Aberdeen Children's Hospital

Sternberg, R.J. (1997) *Thinking Styles*. Cambridge: Cambridge University Press

Sternberg, R.J. and Wagner, R.K. (1991) *MSG Thinking Styles Inventory*. Unpublished manual. Cited in Sternberg, R.J. (1997) *Thinking Styles*. Cambridge: Cambridge University Press

Taylor, M.F. (1998) 'An evaluation of the effects of educational kinesiology (brain gym®) on children manifesting ADHD in a South African context'. Unpublished MPhil dissertation, University of Exeter

Taylor, M.F. (2002) 'Stress-induced atypical brain lateralization in boys with attention-deficit/hyperactivity disorder. Implications for scholastic performance'. Unpublished PhD thesis, University of Western Australia, Perth

Tomlinson, J. (1997) 'Inclusive learning: The report of the committee of inquiry into the post-school education of those with learning difficulties and disabilities in England, 1996', in *European Journal of Special Need Education*, 12(3), 184–96

Tomlinson, C. (1999) *The Differentiated Classroom: Responding to the Needs of All Learners*. Alexandria, VA: Association for Supervision and Curriculum Development

Ulmer, C. and Timothy, M. (2001) 'How does alternative assessment affect teachers' practice two years later?' Paper presented at the 12th European Conference on Reading, Dublin

US Government (2001) Individuals with Disabilities Education Act (IDEA). Washington, DC

Visser, J. (1993) *Differentiation: Making it Work*. Tamworth: NASEN

Vygotsky, L.S. (1962) *Thought and Language*. Cambridge, MA: MIT Press

Vygotsky, L.S. (1978) *Mind in Society: The Development of Higher Psychological Processes*. Cambridge MA: Harvard University Press

Walker Tileston, D. (2005) *Ten Best Teaching Practices. How Brain Research, Learning Styles, and Standards Define Teaching Competencies* (2nd edn). Thousand Oaks, CA: Corwin Press

Watkins, C., Carnell, E., Lodge, C., Wagner, P. and Whalley, C. (2002) 'Effective learning', *Research Matters*, No.5, Summer. NSIN, Institute of Education, London

Wearmouth, J. (2000) *Special Educational Provision; Meeting the Challenges in Schools*. London: Hodder and Stoughton

Wearmouth, J. and Reid, G. (2002) 'Issues for assessment and planning of teaching and learning', in G. Reid and J. Wearmouth (eds) *Dyslexia and Literacy, Theory and Practice*. Chichester: John Wiley and Sons

Wearmouth, J., Soler, J. and Reid, G. (2002) *Meeting Difficulties in Literacy Development; Research, Policy and Practice*. London: RoutledgeFalmer

Wedell, K. (2000) Personal interview, from Wearmouth, J. (2001) 'Inclusion: Changing the variables', in L. Peer and G. Reid (eds) *Dyslexia – Successful Inclusion in the Secondary School*. London: David Fulton

Weedon, C. and Reid, G. (2003) *Special Needs Assessment Portfolio*. London: Hodder and Stoughton

West, T. (1997) *In the Mind's Eye; Visual Thinkers, Gifted People with Dyslexia and Other Learning Difficulties, Computer Images and the Ironies of Creativity* (updated edition). New York: Prometheus Books

Willes, M.J. (1983) *Children into Pupils. A Study of Language in Early Schooling.* London: Routledge and Kegan Paul

Wray, D. (2002) 'Metacognition and literacy', in G. Reid and J. Wearmouth (eds) *Dyslexia and Literacy.* Chichester: John Wiley and Sons

Wray, D. (2004) *The Use of Writing Frames.* (www.warwick.ac.uk/staff/D.J.Wray/Ideas/frames.html)

Wright, C. (2005) *The role of learning styles in writing skills in primary 4.* Unpublished BEd Dissertation. University of Edinburgh, Scotland, UK.

Zimmerman, B.J. (1989) 'Models of self-regulated learning and academic achievement', in B.J. Zimmerman and D.H. Schunk (eds) *Self-regulated Learning and Academic Achievement*, pp1–25. New York; Springer-Verlag

# INDEX

*Added to the page number 'f' denotes a figure and 'g' denotes the glossary.*